INHERITANCE

Minimal Quilts for the Modern Home

RIANE ELISE

INHERITANCE

Minimal Quilts for the Modern Home

Quilts & Patterns | Riane Menardi Morrison
Photography | Austin Day
Photo Styling | Lauren Day
Design & Layout | Erin Menardi
Technical Editing | Yvonne Fuchs
Models | Nadia Allgood, Nyah Noyes, Carol Noyes
Location | Des Moines, Iowa

Inheritance: Minimal Quilts for the Modern Home

Wholesale ordering information
Material Goods | materialgoods.us

ISBN: 978-0-578-41266-5 (paperback)

MATERIALGOODS

materialgoods.us
Crafts & Hobbies | Quilts & Quilting

TABLE OF CONTENTS //

Introduction	7
Materials	8
Techniques	14
General Instructions	32
A Note About Perfection	34

The Patterns

Grid	36
Route	48
First Blush	62
Own	76
Counterpart	90
Prince	104
Companion	118
Guest Pillow	128
Hearth	136
Sway	152

Acknowledgments	164
About the Author	166

inheritance
noun | in·her·i·tance | in-her-e-ten(t)s , -he-re-
: *the acquisition of a possession, condition, trait, skill*
or knowledge from past generations

———————

My grandmother taught me to quilt. It was the summer after college; I was 21, with a fresh journalism degree and no job prospects. While I tried to land on my feet, my grandparents took me in, gave me a bedroom and three meals a day. Between working odd jobs and sending endless applications, I asked my grandmother to teach me to sew. She bought me a pattern, gave me her scrap bins, and together we started a quilt. At the time, I had no idea how that experience would change my life.

For a young woman to learn quilting from her grandmother is to step into a heritage running long and deep through our history. Millions of women have learned this domestic art from their mothers, grandmothers, aunts, sisters, and friends. Quilting offers a means to express oneself, pass the time, form community, make statements, and of course, provide warmth and comfort for our loved ones. It is woven into our past and is one of the few crafts that has been passed down hand to hand, for generations.

Through months of careful instruction, my grandmother passed down her knowledge and passion for quilting to me, as absolutely as any physical good. Together we stepped into the ritual as so many women before us had done. We learned; we talked; and we sewed together. When my grandma taught me to quilt, she gave me a gift, and we continued the tradition.

The quilts in this book are all inspired by that tradition and my idea of home – the people and places that make our lives meaningful. They are modern, looking forward while respecting the past, and they are meant to be made, used and given. Quilters of all skill levels can make these quilts with a few simple tools – a home sewing machine; some fabric and batting; a needle and thread.

For me, quilting was my inheritance, and one I never knew I had until I asked my grandmother to teach me. I believe we're all entitled to learn this art, to make quilts, and to make them our own. Enjoy the journey and happy sewing.

XO,

Riane

Join in on Instagram by following me @riane.elise and posting your work at #inheritancequilts.

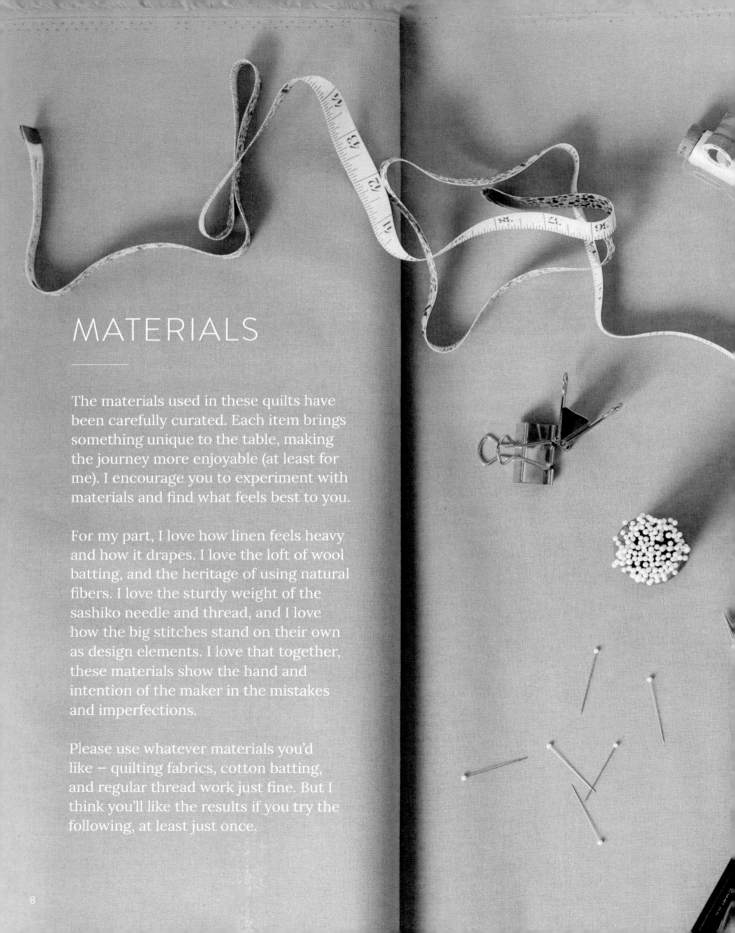

MATERIALS

The materials used in these quilts have been carefully curated. Each item brings something unique to the table, making the journey more enjoyable (at least for me). I encourage you to experiment with materials and find what feels best to you.

For my part, I love how linen feels heavy and how it drapes. I love the loft of wool batting, and the heritage of using natural fibers. I love the sturdy weight of the sashiko needle and thread, and I love how the big stitches stand on their own as design elements. I love that together, these materials show the hand and intention of the maker in the mistakes and imperfections.

Please use whatever materials you'd like – quilting fabrics, cotton batting, and regular thread work just fine. But I think you'll like the results if you try the following, at least just once.

LINEN, COTTON, AND WOOL ARE NATURAL FIBERS THAT ARE AS BEAUTIFUL AS THEY ARE COZY.

Linen & Cotton Fabric

The quilts in this book are made from a blend of 55% linen, 45% cotton fabric. I find this blend to be sturdy and easy to work with, and soft and heavy as a finished quilt. Linen comes from the flax plant and is one of the oldest fibers to be used in textiles. It is known for its strength, cleanliness, absorbency, and long lifespan. The flax fibers relax during the hand quilting process and after use and washing, a linen quilt will become soft, smooth, and very comfortable.

Wool Batting

Wool batting is very lofty, which produces a thick and fluffy quilt. It's the perfect complement to linen because it drapes easily and adds softness. Wool is also warm, complementing the coolness of linen, and despite stereotypes, it's not itchy, especially tucked between the quilt layers. Wool is also a hand quilter's best friend, and I always think it's a joy to work with.

Wide-Eye Needle

If you want to use thick thread for high-contrast hand quilting, you'll need a needle with a wide eye. My favorite needles are sashiko needles, made specifically for sashiko thread. These needles come in a variety of lengths, but I prefer the longest ones. With a long needle, I can make several stitches at a time, which leads to straighter stitches and helps me move faster across the quilt. The large needle and thread also glide smoothly through the loose-weave layers of linen and wool.

Cotton Thread

The thread I used for this book is a 100% cotton thread from Japan called sashiko thread. Sashiko thread has been used in Japan for centuries to strengthen garments and blankets and to add decorative stitches to textiles. It comes in a yarn-like skein, and it's easy to transport and work with. The thickness of the thread adds weight, dimension and interest to a quilt, and the stitches stand on their own as design elements.

Other Helpful Materials

- Large cutting mat
- Quilting ruler
- Yardstick or tape measure
- Big cutting table, workspace, or a nice clean floor

- Walking foot
- Rotary cutter
- Fabric scissors & snips
- Pencil or chalk for marking
- Painters tape

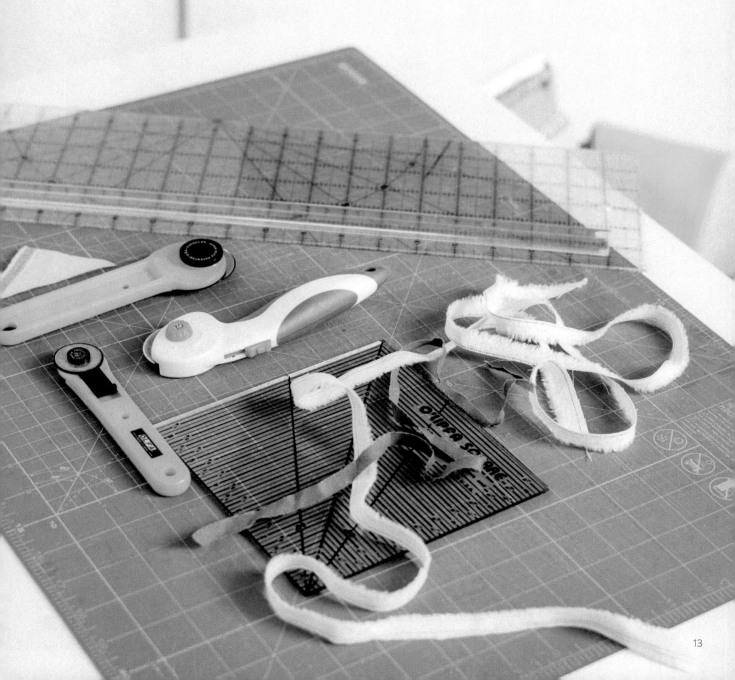

TECHNIQUES

Hand Quilting

All of the quilts in this book have been hand quilted. When we were making our first quilt together (a queen), my grandmother challenged me to hand quilt it, saying I'd love it that much more. I tried, but the traditional needle and small stitches didn't work for me. I just wanted the quilt to be done, and hand quilting wasn't fast, easy, or fun.

Once I found the right materials, however, everything changed. Now I finish every quilt by hand. I love the aesthetic of large, high-contrast hand quilting, as well as the meditative quality of it. By individually making each stitch as a design element, the quilt becomes completely my own. I feel connected to each decision that goes into the quilt, and finishing by hand helps infuse intention and meaning into my work. If you've never hand quilted before, I encourage you to try it at least once, and see if it changes anything for you about quiltmaking.

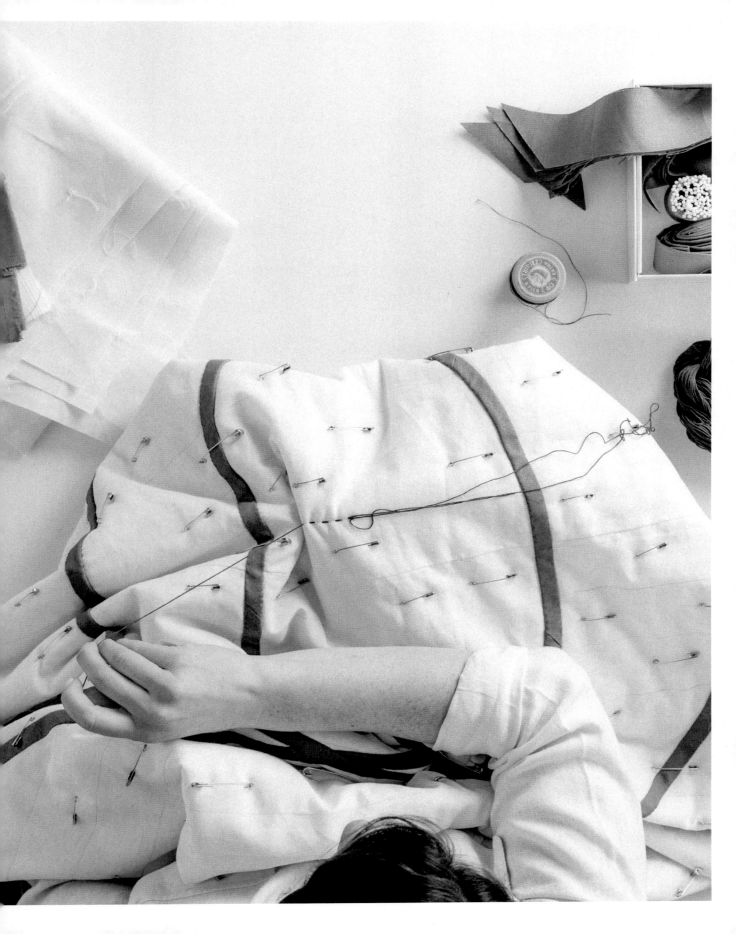

Making the Sashiko Braid

Sashiko thread is easiest to work with when it is woven into a braid, rather than using the skein that it comes packaged in. Follow these steps to form the braid.

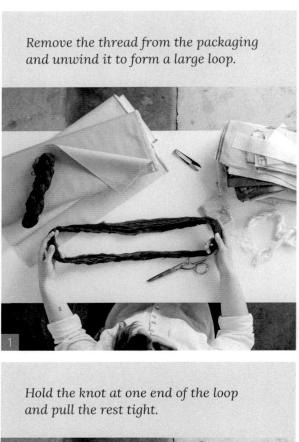

Remove the thread from the packaging and unwind it to form a large loop.

Find the knotted end (usually this is a small loop of thread that holds the skein together).

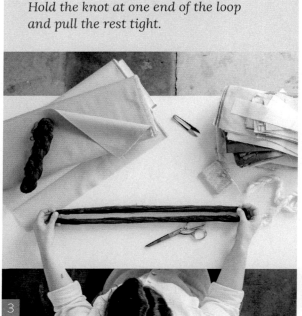

Hold the knot at one end of the loop and pull the rest tight.

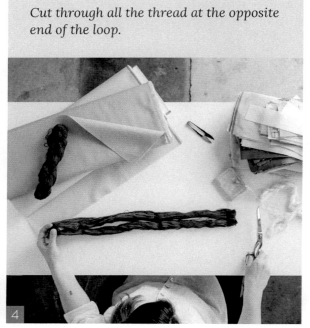

Cut through all the thread at the opposite end of the loop.

Keeping the loop at the top, separate the strands into three sections.

Braid the sections.

WHEN YOU PREPARE THE SKEIN IN THIS WAY, EACH STRAND IS THE PERFECT LENGTH FOR HAND QUILTING.

At the end, snip a piece of thread from the bottom and tie the braid.

When you're ready to sew, pull a strand out from the top of the braid.

Hand Quilting: Stitching

Tie a double knot at one end of your thread and thread the other. Insert the needle into the back of your quilt and up through the front. Pull tight.

To hide the knot, carefully pop it through the backing to the batting layer.

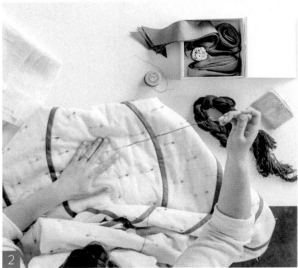

Make your stitches by inserting the needle into the fabric through all layers. Accordion the fabric over your needle using your left hand (if you're right-handed). I keep my left hand under the quilt. Load about 3-5 stitches on the needle at a time, making the stitches on top slightly longer than the stitches underneath.

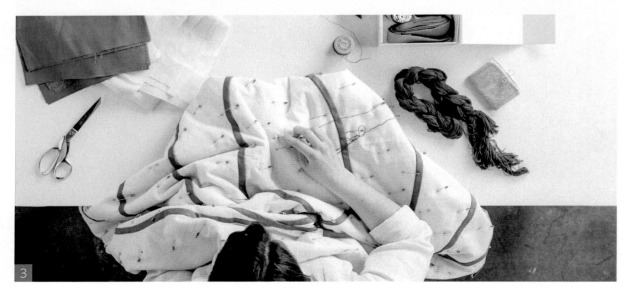

When you're ready, hold the quilt in one hand and the needle in the other and pull the needle and thread all the way through. Smooth out any puckers. Then begin the accordion again, working across the quilt.

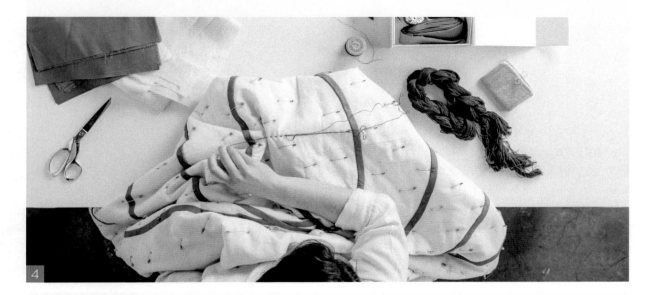

When you reach the end of your thread, pull the needle through to the back and tie a knot close to the backing. Insert your needle into the sandwich and, pop the knot through to the batting layer once again. Trim the tail and carry on until you've finished the quilt.

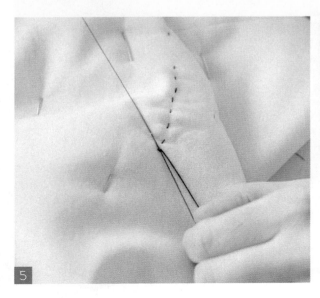

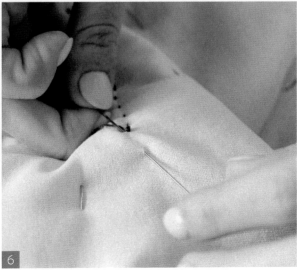

Motifs & Marking

Deciding on a quilting motif deserves careful consideration. When deciding how to quilt, think about how your stitches can inform the piecing and add depth and dimension to the overall quilt. Straight lines can accentuate the geometry of a quilt design, where curves could soften it. I try to choose a design that will showcase the stitches without competing with the other visual features. I usually echo my seams or quilt perpendicular to them to continue the conversation with the angles I've already created. The quilts in the book are quilted about 1 ½"–3" apart, but be sure to follow the quilting guidelines specified for your batting.

When you're ready to mark, use a lead or chalk pencil to draw your lines. I usually use a ruler so my lines are straight and evenly spaced, but you can also draw them freehand. Pencil and chalk can both be easily erased from linen fabric, so you can always adjust.

Hand Appliqué

Some of the quilts in this book are made with appliqué, which simply means to sew fabric pieces on top of each other. Appliqué is useful for creating shapes that are difficult to piece (like the large rings in Counterpart, pg. 90). I appliqué by hand most often, and this is my favorited method.

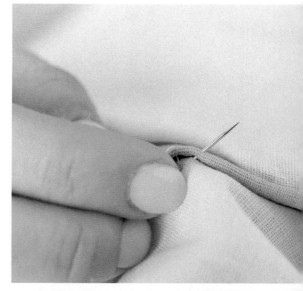

1. Start with a fine thread in the same color as your appliqué piece (the top one). This helps your stitches blend in. You'll also want a thin needle, like a standard hand sewing or appliqué needle. Knot your thread a few times and thread the needle.

2. Align your appliqué piece on the fabric where you want to attach it (it's helpful to mark the lines — see the marking workshop for Counterpart on pg. 96). You can pin or thread baste the appliqué piece to the background fabric, but it's not necessary.

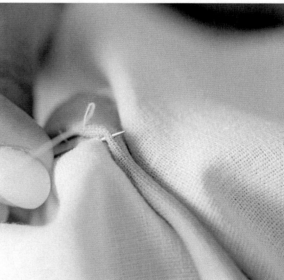

3. Bring your needle and thread up through the background fabric and through the folded edge of the appliqué piece. Catch just a little bit of the appliqué edge and insert your needle down into the background fabric again. Bring it up through both layers to make your next stitch, then back down through the background.

4. Continue on like this, catching the edge of your appliqué fabric and making tiny stitches (I sew mine about ¼"). Readjust as needed to make sure you're following your marked lines.

Finishing Your Quilt

Backing

The backing is the bottom layer of a quilt. Some of the quilts in this book are double-sided, meaning you can choose to piece a backing just like you would the quilt top. The double-sided quilts can also be made with a traditional backing — usually a solid piece of fabric or two large pieces sewn together.

To sew a traditional backing, you should select a backing fabric that complements the front. Remember that your backing should be at least 4" larger than your top (at least 2" of overhang on each side). Usually it's best to cut the length of fabric to a few inches longer than the length of your quilt top. If needed, cut a second length of fabric and sew these two pieces together to make a wider backing.

You can also buy wide fabric made specifically for backing, or you can piece a backing with scraps from another project.

Making Double-Sided Quilts

For double-sided quilts, your top and backing will be about the same size. This just means you need to pay more attention to lining up the layers — but don't worry. The *Inheritance* quilts that are reversible can also be trimmed without affecting the design.

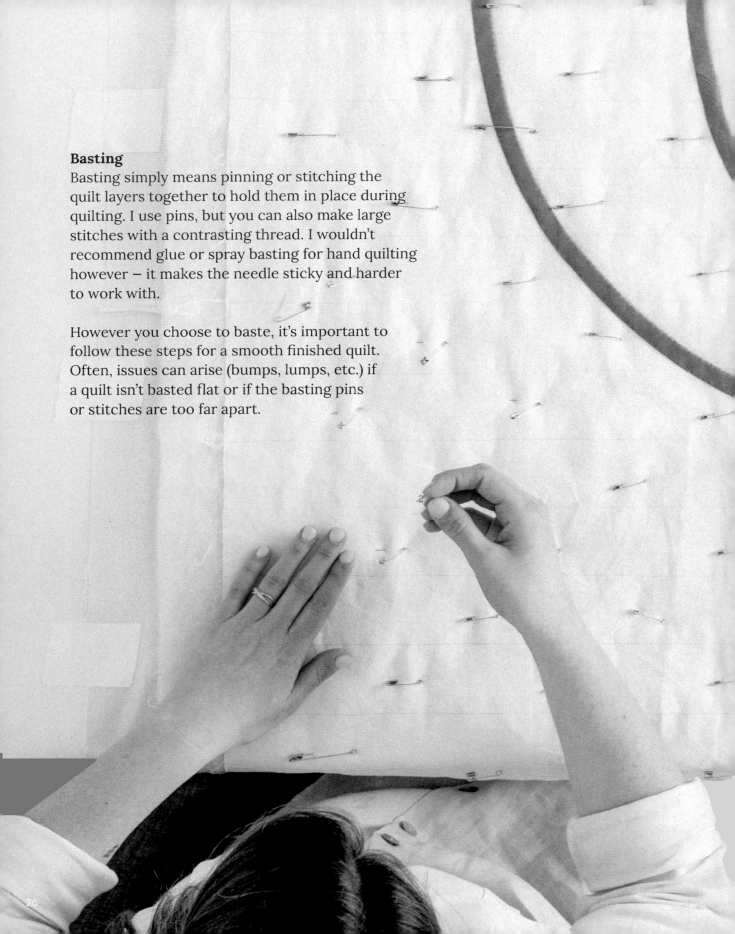

Basting

Basting simply means pinning or stitching the quilt layers together to hold them in place during quilting. I use pins, but you can also make large stitches with a contrasting thread. I wouldn't recommend glue or spray basting for hand quilting however — it makes the needle sticky and harder to work with.

However you choose to baste, it's important to follow these steps for a smooth finished quilt. Often, issues can arise (bumps, lumps, etc.) if a quilt isn't basted flat or if the basting pins or stitches are too far apart.

BASTING IS EASIEST ON A BIG TABLE, BUT A HARDWOOD FLOOR WORKS WELL FOR LARGE QUILTS.

1. Choose your basting space. It should be a flat, hard surface, and big enough for your whole quilt (or most of it). A hardwood floor or large table work well.

> **TIP //** *If pin basting, there's a chance you could scratch the surface, so either choose a surface you don't mind scratching, or lay down a protective layer like paper or plastic. Use tape or binding clips to hold the protective layer taut.*

2. Iron the layers so they're as flat as possible. You can even iron the batting (though with wool, just hover a steam iron over the top to smooth).

3. Place your backing right-side down on your basting surface. Use a no-residue tape to hold the whole backing down as flat as possible. Start on one side, tape, then pull the other side taut and tape. Work your way across the remaining sides. If you're working on a table, you can also use large binder clips to hold the backing to your surface.

4. Lay your batting on top of the backing, smoothing any wrinkles. Finally, lay your quilt top over the top, right-side up.

> **NOTE //** *This is when I like to mark my quilting lines. I find that the batting helps keep the quilt top from sliding. Mark any lines you need before basting.*

5. Next, you'll baste.

   a. **For pin basting:** *Place your pins between and around your marking lines so they don't get in your way during quilting. Place them at least 2"-3" apart so your layers don't shift. I like to place all my pins first and then close them at the end.*

   b. **For thread basting:** *Choose a contrasting color so you can easily remove the thread later. Using a curved needle or a long standard needle, make large stitches through all the layers of your quilt. Your stitches can be 1"-2" long, but make sure to baste about 2"-3" apart so your layers don't shift. Don't worry about tying your ends. Leaving long tails will help in removing the stitches later.*

Now you're ready to quilt! Visit pg. 18 to review the hand quilting process.

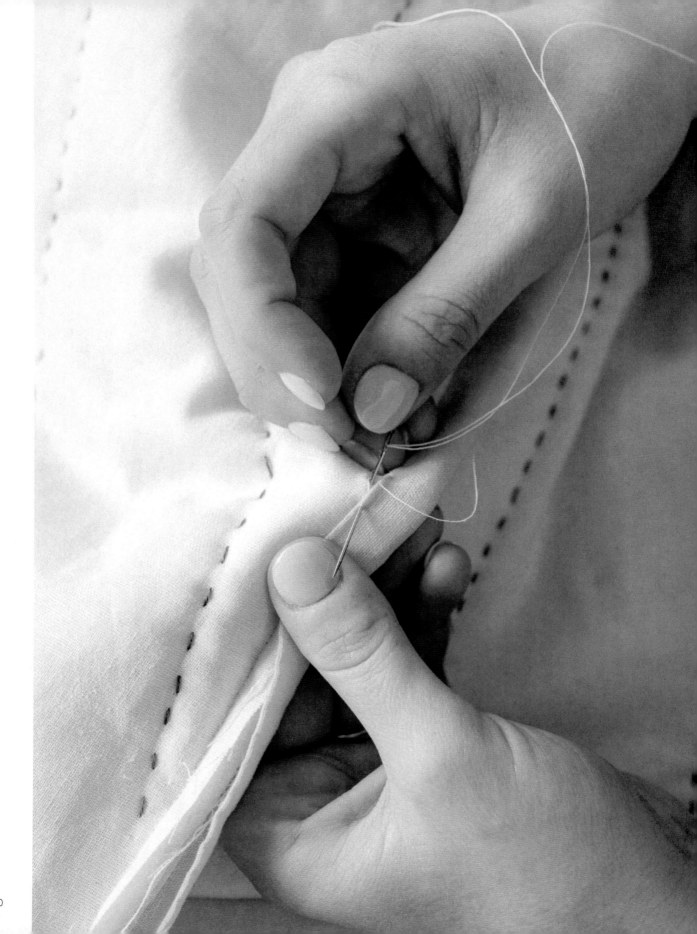

Binding

After quilting, you'll bind your quilt to cover the raw edges and finish the quilt. The quilts in this book use 2 ½" binding strips to accommodate the bulkiness of wool and linen. Here's my favorite way to bind:

1. Cut the number of binding strips required (this is indicated in the quilt pattern). Sew the binding strips together on the bias or straight across. Press all your seams open to reduce bulk.

2. Next, press your binding strip in half lengthwise so the strip is 1 ¼" wide.

3. Place the binding strip on top of your quilt, raw edges together. Using a walking foot on your machine, start stitching about 4" from the top of the strip.

4. Sew the binding to the quilt using a standard ¼" seam. When you come to a corner, backstitch ¼" from the edge and cut your threads. Remove your quilt and pull the binding strip straight up (Diagram 1). Next, pull your binding straight down and fold it so the folded edge matches with the top line of your quilt (Diagram 2). Start stitching again ¼" from the top edge, and continue on this side.

5. Continue stitching the binding in this manner until you are 6"-8" away from where you started. Snip the threads and remove your quilt.

6. Lay out the quilt with the two binding tails face up in front of you. Trim so they overlap by ¼". Sew these binding ends right-sides together using a ¼" seam. Press open. The binding should now be exactly the right size for your quilt.

7. Stitch the rest of your binding down, backstitching at the end of your seam to finish.

8. Fold the finished edge of your binding over to the back, and stitch it down using a small, invisible stitch (shown left).

Diagram 1

Diagram 2

General Instructions

- Please read through all instructions before starting a pattern.

- Standard width of fabric is assumed to be 42" without selvage.

- "Width of fabric" is abbreviated as "WOF."

- All of the quilts in this book use a ¼" seam as the standard. Any other seam allowance will be noted in the instructions.

- "Half-square triangle" is abbreviated as "HST."

- "Half-rectangle triangle" is abbreviated as "HRT."

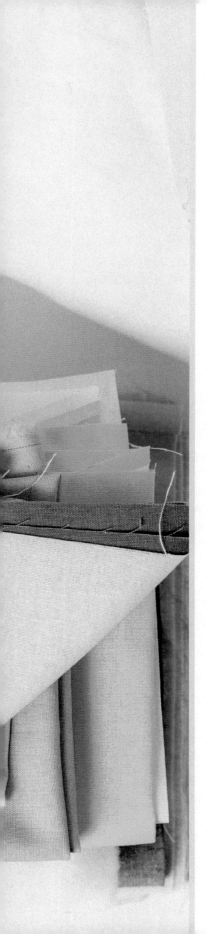

Terms

- **_Batting_** | The layer between your quilt top and quilt back

- **_Bind_** | To finish a quilt so it has no raw edges

- **_Double-Sided Quilt_** | A reversible quilt, or one where both sides are pieced as quilt tops

- **_Half-Square Rectangle_** | A rectangle unit that is pieced together using two tall right triangles

- **_Half-Square Triangle_** | A square unit that is pieced together using two isosceles right triangles

- **_Press Open_** | After sewing, using an iron to separate the seams on the wrong side so they lay open and flat

- **_Quilt_** | A blanket made of three layers held together by stitches covering the whole surface (quilting)

- **_Quilt Back or Backing_** | The bottom layer of a quilt

- **_Quilt Top_** | The top layer of a quilt

- **_Quilt Sandwich_** | The three layers of a quilt (quilt top, batting, backing)

- **_Quilting_** | The stitching that holds all the layers in a quilt together

- **_Sashiko_** (needle, thread) | Traditional Japanese materials that are used to create decorative and functional stitches on clothing, blankets, pillows, etc.

- **_Seam_** | The join between two pieces of fabric

- **_Seam Allowance_** | The area between the stitch and the edge of the fabric; in quilting, the standard seam allowance is ¼"

- **_Square Up_** | To straighten the quilt edges and corners or trim to a certain size

- **_Trim_** | To remove any ragged or unstraight edges with a rotary cutter

- **_Width of Fabric_** | The full width of fabric once it is unfolded from the bolt

A Note About Perfection

There is no perfect quilt in this book, and you likely won't make a perfect quilt from these patterns. (If you do, I salute you!) Just remember that each quilt is made by hand, and it's only meant to be functional, lasting, and something you enjoy – it doesn't need to be technically perfect.

In this book we'll work with bias seams, large pieces, hand quilting and linen fabric (which can be a bit stretchier than cotton). This combination makes it hard to finish a quilt perfectly. The materials may stretch, your seams may be a bit off, and the quilt may not be exactly straight in the end. That's okay.

I give you permission to cut yourself a break, recognize the beauty in each mistake and imperfection, and make a decision on how to move forward with what you have – no seam ripping, restitching, or trimming required.

Here are some of my favorite ways to deal with mistakes and imperfections.

- **Overhanging edges:** Don't fret, just trim the excess.

- **Long borders, strips and sashing:** Sew the pieces together first, then trim to size. Many of the quilts in this book have pieces that can be trimmed after piecing.

- **Wonky seams:** For me, ripping stitches is always a last resort. If the seam is only slightly off, you can probably move on without affecting the finished quilt.

- **Unsquare quilts:** You can trim the quilt to square by using the corner of a table to line up your edges; mark where you need to cut, then carefully trim the quilt. You can also can embrace the unsquare quilt by quilting and binding it as is. Some of my favorite quilts aren't squared up; they have their own unique beauty.

GRID

Grid

This quilt is based on my idea of home. I designed and made Grid shortly after my wedding, when I was reflecting on what it means to be "at home." Grid was inspired by the foundation of a house, and the layers of grids in the quilting also represent the structured support systems of being home – both physically and emotionally. I like the simplicity in the design and the layers of contrasting grids that run throughout the piecing and the stitching.

GRID // *Materials*

	WHITE	GRAY	BACKING	BINDING
King: 90" x 102"	2 yards	7 yards	8 yards	1 yard (10 strips)
Full: 60" x 66"	2 yards	2 yards	3 ¾ yards	¾ yard (7 strips)
Throw: 45" x 51"	¾ yard	2 ¼ yards	3 yards	½ yard (6 strips)

Cutting instructions are the same for king and full sizes except where noted.
Throw instructions are indicated in parenthesis: king/full (throw).

Cutting Instructions

	WHITE	GRAY
King/Full	**(17) 3 ½" x WOF strips, subcut into:** • (10) 3 ½" x 30 ½" (White D) • (14) 3 ½" x 14" (White B) • (6) 3 ½" x 12 ½" (White C) • (8) 3 ½" x 6 ½" (White A)	**(4) 7" x WOF strips, subcut into:** • (12) 7" x 14" (Gray B) **(5) 6½" x WOF strips, subcut into:** • (4) 6 ½" x 26" (Gray C) • (12) 6 ½" x 7" (Gray A) **(4) 18 ½" x WOF (Gray E) - king only** **(6) 15 ½" x WOF (Gray F) - king only**
Throw	**(9) 2" x WOF strips, subcut into:** • (5) 2" x 30 ½" (White D) • (14) 2" x 7 ¼" (White B) • (6) 2" x 6 ½" (White C) • (8) 2" x 3 ½" (White A)	**(3) 3 ¾" x WOF strips, subcut into:** • (12) 3 ¾" x 7 ¼" (Gray B) • (12) 3 ¾" x 3 ½" (Gray A) **(2) 3 ½" x WOF strips, subcut into:** • (4) 3 ½" x 13 ¼" (Gray C) **(2) 9 ½" x WOF strips (Gray E)** **(4) 8" x WOF strips (Gray F)**

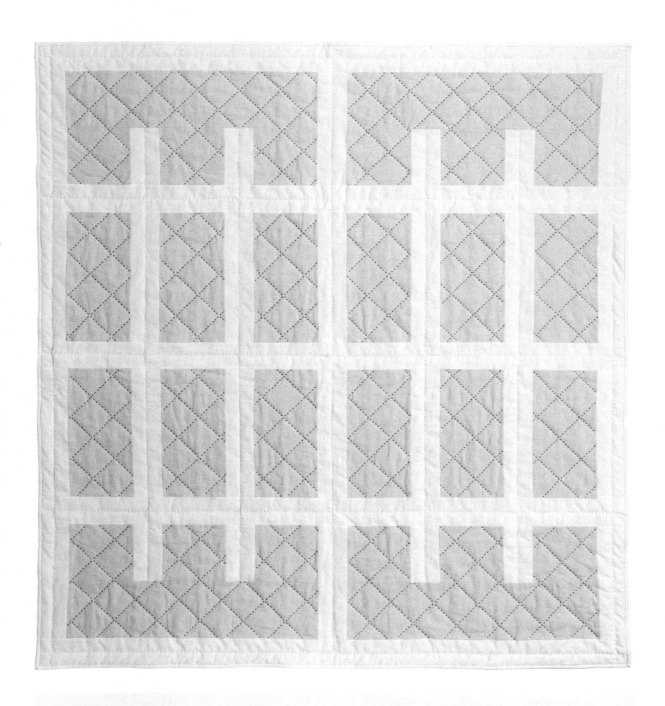

QUILTING MOTIF // *Since this quilt has a strong grid structure in the piecing, I wanted to create a secondary motif in the background that continues the conversation. So I chose a cross-hatch quilting pattern with 45° lines running across the entire background area of the quilt. I love how it adds both rigidity and movement to the design.*

Assembly

1. Sew a White A rectangle to a Gray A rectangle as shown in Diagram 1. Press seam open. Repeat to make eight subunits. Subunit should measure 6 ½" x 10" (3 ½" x 5 ¼"). Note that you will have four Gray A rectangles remaining to use in the next step.

2. Arrange two White and Gray A subunits from Step 1 with a Gray A rectangle into strips as shown in Diagram 2. Sew these sections together to form four A strips, pressing seams open. Set these A strips aside. Strip A should measure 6 ½" x 26" (3 ½" x 13 ¼").

3. Using seven White B and six Gray B rectangles, make a long B strip as shown in Diagram 3. Press seams open. Repeat with the remaining B rectangles to make a second B strip. Trim edges so they are neat and straight. Strip B should measure 14" x 60 ½" (7 ¼" x 30 ½").

4. Sew two White D rectangles together along their shortest sides, and press open. Set aside. Repeat with the remaining D pieces to make five D strips. Strip D should measure 3 ½" x 60 ½" (2" x 30 ½"). *

*Skip this step if making the throw size

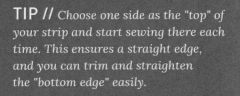

TIP // *Choose one side as the "top" of your strip and start sewing there each time. This ensures a straight edge, and you can trim and straighten the "bottom edge" easily.*

King/Throw

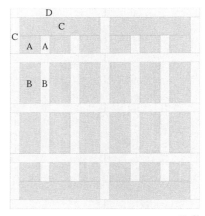

Full

Diagram 1

A STRIP

Diagram 2

B STRIP

Diagram 3   Diagram 4

5. Sew a Gray C rectangle to an A strip as shown in Diagram 4, pressing seam open. Repeat this step three more times with the remaining fabric. Subunit should measure 12 ½" x 26" (6 ½" x 13 ¼").

6. Use two subunits from Step 5 and three White C rectangles to create a C strip as shown in Diagram 5. Press seams open. Create two. Strip C should measure 12 ½" x 60 ½" (6 ½" x 30 ½").

7. Sew two White D strips from Step 4 to the top and bottom of your C strip as shown in Diagram 6. Repeat to make two subunits that measure 18 ½" x 60 ½" (9 ½" x 30 ½").

8. Sew the remaining White D strip between the two B strips as shown in Diagram 7. Pin generously from the middle out, making sure to line up the white lines. Press seams open. Subunit should measure 30 ½" x 60 ½" (15 ½" x 30 ½").

PRESSING OPEN //
I like to press open after sewing each seam to reduce bulk. This makes it easier to move through the layers during hand quilting.

TIP // Use the center seams in your White D strips as guides to center up the B strips, lining them up from the middle out. These seams will help as you construct the middle section of your quilt. Pin the center seams first and pin outward to keep everything in line.

C STRIP

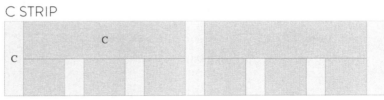

Diagram 5

Diagram 6

Diagram 7

Assemble the Middle Section

9. Assemble the three middle section pieces from Steps 7 and 8 as shown in Diagram 8. Press open. If you're making the full size, this is your last step! This section should measure 66 ½" x 60 ½" (33 ½" x 30 ½").

Diagram 8

Assemble the Borders
For king and throw sizes only

10. Sew two Gray E pieces together end to end to make an E border piece. Repeat to make another. Trim to the average measured width of the middle section. The E border should measure approximately 18 ½" x 60 ½" (9 ½" x 30 ½"). *
    * Skip this step for throw size.

11. Sew three (two for throw) Gray F pieces together end to end to make an F border piece. Repeat to make another.

Assemble the Quilt Top

12. Sew the E border to the top and bottom of the middle section (Diagram 9). Press seams open.

13. Trim the F borders to the average measured height, approximately 15 ½" x 102 ½" (8" x 51 ½").

14. Sew the F border to the left and right as shown in Diagram 9. Press seams open. Quilt top should measure 90 ½" x 102 ½" (45" x 51 ½").

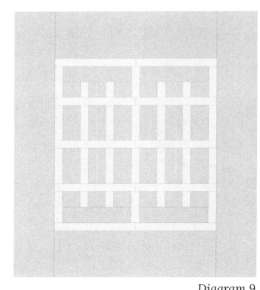

Diagram 9

MOST QUILTS THROUGHOUT HISTORY HAVE BEEN PIECED OR FINISHED BY HAND. LOOK CLOSELY AT AN OLD QUILT AND YOU CAN CLEARLY SEE THE HAND OF THE MAKER. EACH QUILT TELLS A STORY.

Route

Route was inspired by a race arrow I saw on the bike trail near my house. I walk that path almost every day with my dog, but one morning I noticed a small sticker on the pavement. It was pointing in the direction we were going – deeper into the woods and further from home. That arrow was the inspiration for this quilt, and it reminds me to stay the course, keep making, and keep exploring.

ROUTE SIDE 1 // *Materials*

	GRAY	WHITE	BACKING	BINDING
Crib: 36" x 41"	½ yard	1 ½ yards	1 ¼ yards	½ yard (4 strips)
Throw: 54" x 61"	1 yard	3 yards	3 ½ yards	½ yard (6 strips)
Twin: 72" x 82"	1 ¼ yards	4 ½ yards	5 yards	¾ yard (8 strips)

This quilt is double-sided, and you can use the Side 2 instructions on page 55 for the other side.
If you'd rather make a traditional quilt, the backing yardage is indicated above.
Instructions are written twin (throw, crib). Variations are marked with an asterisk.

Side 1

Side 2

QUILTING MOTIF //
I reinforced the direction of the arrows with simple, straight-line quilting. The thread color changes with the fabric to add interest.

Cutting Instructions

	GRAY	WHITE	
Crib	**FOR GEESE UNITS** **(2) 4 ½" x WOF strips, subcut into:** • (5) 4 ½" x 9 ½" (A) • (5) 4 ½" x 2 ½" (B) **(1) 2 ½" x WOF strip, subcut into:** • (10) 2 ½" x 2 ½" (C)	**FOR GEESE UNITS** **(2) 2 ½" x WOF strips, subcut into:** • (5) 2 ½" x 4 ½" (B) • (10) 2 ½" x 2 ½" (C)	**FOR BACKGROUND** **(1) 17 ½" x WOF strip, subcut into:** • (1) 17 ½" x 41 ½" (H) **(1) 10 ½" x WOF strip, subcut into:** • (1) 10 ½" x 19 ½" (F) • (1) 5 ½" x 19 ½" (G) **(1) 6 ½" x WOF strip, subcut into:** • (1) 6 ½" x 26 ½" (E) **(2) 2" x WOF strips, subcut into:** • (4) 2" x 13 ½" (D)
Throw	**FOR GEESE UNITS** **(3) 6 ½" x WOF strips, subcut into:** • (5) 6 ½" x 14 ½" (A) • (5) 6 ½" x 3 ½" (B) **(1) 3 ½" x WOF strip, subcut into:** • (10) 3 ½" x 3 ½" (C)	**FOR GEESE UNITS** **(2) 3 ½" x WOF strips, subcut into:** • (5) 3 ½" x 6 ½" (B) • (10) 3 ½" x 3 ½" (C)	**FOR BACKGROUND** **(2) 25 ½" x WOF strips (H)** **(1) 15 ½" x WOF strip, subcut into:** • (1) 15 ½" x 29 ½" (F) **(1) 9 ½" x WOF strip, subcut into:** • (1) 9 ½" x 39 ½" (E) **(1) 7 ½" x WOF strip, subcut into:** • (1) 7 ½" x 29 ½" (G) **(2) 2 ¾" x WOF strips, subcut into:** • (4) 2 ¾" x 20 ½" (D)
Twin	**FOR GEESE UNITS** **(3) 8 ½" x WOF strips, subcut into:** • (5) 8 ½" x 18 ½" (A) • (5) 8 ½" x 4 ½" (B) **(1) 4 ½" x WOF strip, subcut into:** • (10) 4 ½" x 4 ½" (C) *	**FOR GEESE UNITS** **(3) 4 ½" x WOF strips, subcut into:** • (5) 4 ½" x 8 ½" (B) • (10) 4 ½" x 4 ½" (C) ** You can cut nine squares from one strip of fabric, so use the scrap from the previous step to cut the last one.*	**FOR BACKGROUND** **(2) 34 ½" x WOF strips (H)** **(1) 20 ½" x WOF strip, subcut into:** • (1) 20 ½" x 38 ½" (F) **(2) 12 ½" x WOF strips (E)** **(1) 10 ½" x WOF strip, subcut into:** • (1) 10 ½" x 38 ½" (G) **(4) 3 ½" x WOF strips, subcut into:** • (4) 3 ½" x 26 ½" (D)

Assembly

Make the Gray Flying Geese

1. Take your gray B rectangles and white C squares. Mark a line on the wrong side of all your C squares diagonally from one corner to the other.

2. Place a marked white C square right sides together on the right side of a gray B rectangle as shown in Diagram 1. Sew on the drawn line. Trim the corner, leaving a ¼" seam allowance (Diagram 2). Press open (Diagram 3).

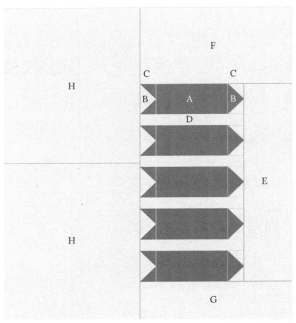

Route Side 1

Diagram 1

Diagram 2

Diagram 3

3. Lay another marked White C square on top of the flying geese unit right sides together as shown in Diagram 4. Sew on the drawn line and trim, leaving a ¼" seam allowance (Diagram 5). Press open to finish your flying geese unit. It should measure 8 ½" x 4 ½" (6 ½" x 3 ½", 4 ½" x 2 ½") (Diagram 6).

TIP // *Sew from the corner to the middle of your goose for best results.*

4. Repeat Steps 2–3 four more times to create a total of five gray flying geese units.

Diagram 4

Diagram 5

Diagram 6

Make the White Flying Geese

5. To make the white flying geese unites, follow the same process (Steps 2–4), but this time use the white B rectangles and the gray C squares. Make a total of five white flying geese units measuring 8 ½" x 4 ½" (6 ½" x 3 ½", 4 ½" x 2 ½").

Make the Gray Arrows

6. Using one gray and one white flying geese unit, arrange them on either side of a gray A rectangle as shown in Diagram 7. Sew these together and press seams open to complete one arrow. Repeat this step four more times to make a total of five gray arrow units. Gray arrows should measure 8 ½" x 26 ½" (6 ½" x 20 ½", 4 ½" x 13 ½").

7. Take your white D rectangles and arrange them with the arrow units as shown in Diagram 8. Sew the rows together and press open. Subunit should measure 26 ½" x 52 ½" (20 ½" x 39 ½", 13 ½" x 26 ½").

Diagram 7

8. Take your two E WOF strips* and trim the selvages. Sew the strips together end to end to form a long strip that is 12 ½" wide. Trim to the average measured height of the subunit from Step 7, approximately 12 ½" x 52 ½". Sew the E rectangle to the right side of your arrow unit (Diagram 9). Subunit should measure 38 ½" x 52 ½" (29 ½" x 39 ½", 19 ½" x 26 ½").

*For the throw and crib size, you already have a single E rectangle and do not need to sew two pieces together.

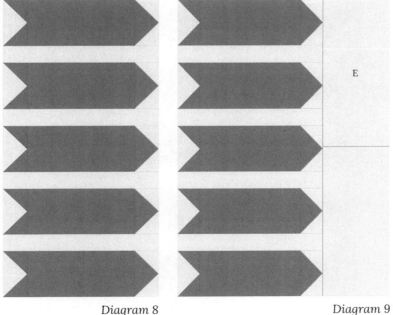

E

Diagram 10

Diagram 8

Diagram 9

TIP // *Sew the pieces together with the arrow unit on top, so you can see the seams and points in your gray flying geese. This way you can guide your needle to intersect with the top of the points so they don't get buried (Diagram 10).*

9. Sew the F rectangle to the top of the arrow unit as shown in Diagram 11. Press seams open. Subunit should measure 38 ½" x 72 ½" (29 ½" x 54 ½", 19 ½" x 36 ½").

10. Sew the G rectangle the bottom of the arrow unit as shown in Diagram 12. Press seams open. Subunit should measure 38 ½" x 82 ½" (29 ½" x 61 ½", 19 ½" x 41 ½").

11. Take your two H WOF strips* and trim the selvages. Sew the strips together end to end to form a long strip that is 34 ½" (25 ½") wide. Trim to the average measured height of the subunit from Step 10, approximately 34 ½" x 82 ½" (25 ½" x 61 ½"). Pin the H rectangle generously to the left side of your quilt and stitch in place (Diagram 13). Press seam open to finish. Quilt top should measure approximately 72 ½" x 82 ½" (54 ½" x 61 ½", 36 ½" x 41 ½").

*For the crib size, you already have a single H rectangle and do not need to sew two pieces together.

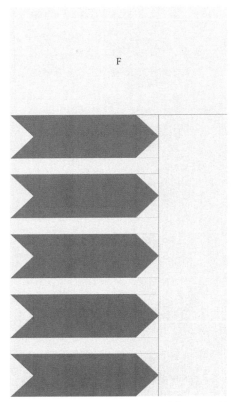

Diagram 11

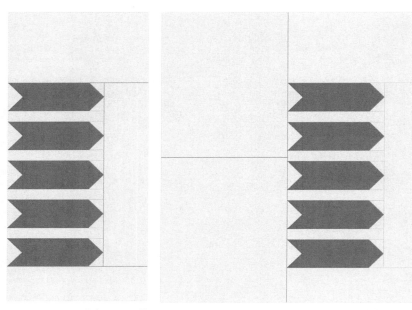

Diagram 12

Diagram 13

TIP // All this negative space makes Route a fun one to quilt. As you finish the top, think about how to create movement and lead the eye around the quilt. View it from a distance to get inspired!

ROUTE SIDE 2 // *Materials*

	GRAY	WHITE	BACKING	BINDING
Crib: 36" x 41"	¾ yard	1 ¼ yards	1 ¼ yards	½ yard (4 strips)
Throw: 54" x 61"	¾ yard	3 ¼ yards	3 ½ yards	½ yard (6 strips)
Twin: 72" x 82"	1 yard	4 ¼ yards	5 yards	¾ yard (8 strips)

This quilt is double-sided, and you can use the Side 1 instructions on page 50 for the other side. If you'd rather make a traditional quilt, the backing yardage is indicated above. Instructions are written twin (throw, crib). Variations are marked with an asterisk.

Cutting Instructions

	GRAY	WHITE
Crib	**(1) 10 ½" x WOF strip, subcut into:** • (1) 10 ½" x 21 ½" (A) • (2) 5 ½" x 5 ½" (C)	**(2) 16" x WOF strips, subcut into:** • (2) 16" x 36 ½" (E) **(1) 10 ½" x WOF strip, subcut into:** • (1) 10 ½" x 10 ½" (D) • (1) 10 ½" x 5 ½" (B)
Throw	**(1) 15 ½" x WOF strip, subcut into:** • (1) 15 ½" x 32" (A) **(1) 8" x WOF strips, subcut into:** • (2) 8" x 8" (C)	**(4) 23 ½" x WOF strips (E)** **(1) 15 ½" x WOF strip, subcut into:** • (1) 15 ½" x 15 ½" (D) • (1) 15 ½" x 8" (B)
Twin	**(1) 20 ½" x WOF strip, subcut into:** • (1) 20 ½" x 42 ½" (A) **(1) 10 ½" x WOF strip, subcut into:** • (2) 10 ½" x 10 ½" (C)	**(4) 31 ½" x WOF strips (E)** **(1) 20 ½" x WOF strip, subcut into:** • (1) 20 ½" x 20 ½" (D) • (1) 20 ½" x 10 ½" (B)

Make the White Flying Geese

1. Draw diagonal lines on the wrong sides of your gray C squares from corner to corner. Layer a gray C square right sides together on the right side of a white B rectangle, as shown in Diagram 14. Sew on the drawn line. Trim the corner off, leaving a ¼" seam allowance from your seam (Diagram 15). Press open (Diagram 16).

2. Place a second gray C square right sides together on the left side of your flying geese unit as shown in Diagram 17. Sew on the drawn line, and trim the corner away, leaving ¼" seam allowance (Diagram 18). Press open to finish your flying geese unit. It should measure 20 ½" x 10 ½" (15 ½" x 8", 10 ½" x 5 ½") (Diagram 19).

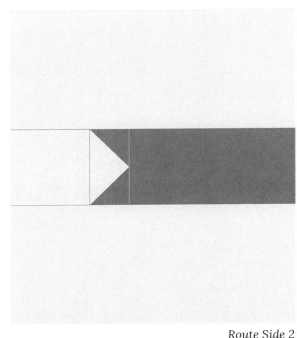

Route Side 2

TIP // *Sew from the corner to the middle of your goose for best results.*

3. Sew your flying geese unit to your D square as shown in Diagram 20. Pin generously to avoid stretching. Press seam open. Subunit should measure 30 ½" x 20 ½" (23" x 15 ½", 15 ½" x 10 ½").

4. Sew your flying geese unit from Step 3 to the gray A rectangle as shown in Diagram 21. Press seam open. Subunit should measure 72 ½" x 20 ½" (54 ½" x 15 ½", 36 ½" x 10 ½").

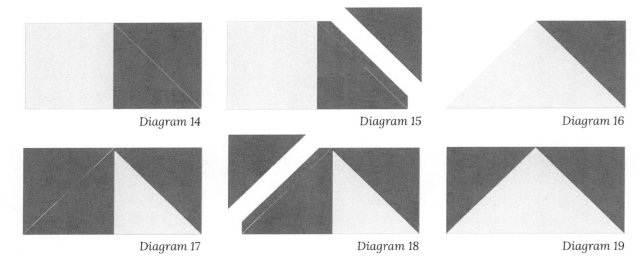

Diagram 14   *Diagram 15*   *Diagram 16*

Diagram 17   *Diagram 18*   *Diagram 19*

Borders

5. Trim the selvages off your four E WOF strips.* Sew two strips together end to end to form a long strip that is 31 ½" (23 ½") wide. Trim to the average measured width of the subunit from Step 5, approximately 31 ½" x 72 ½" (23 ½" x 54 ½"). Repeat to make a second E rectangle with the remaining two pieces.

   For the crib size, you already have a single E rectangle and do not need to sew two pieces together.

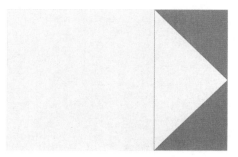

Diagram 20

6. Sew your E rectangles on the top and bottom of your flying geese unit from Step 5. Press seams open (Diagram 22). Quilt top should measure 72 ½" x 82 ½" (54 ½" x 61 ½", 36 ½" x 41 ½").

Diagram 21

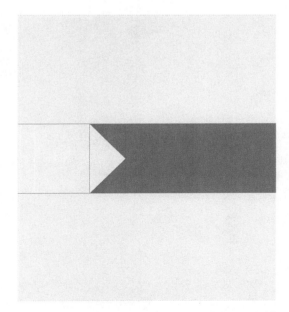

DOUBLE-SIDED QUILTS //

Since this quilt is double-sided, you can choose to leave Side 2 slightly larger than Side 1 and trim after quilting if you prefer. If you trim Side 2 to size now, be careful during the basting process to line up the front and back as neatly as possible. (But don't worry! This quilt has lots of negative space on both sides, so you can trim without affecting the design.) Refer to page 26 for more on basting.

Diagram 22

QUILT DENSELY FOR A STURDY, DURABLE QUILT. QUILT LOOSELY FOR A PLUSH QUILT WITH LOTS OF DRAPE. BOTH WILL CONTINUE TO SOFTEN WITH AGE AND WASHING.

FIRST BLUSH

First Blush

This litte quilt began as a study in contrast using traditional half-square triangles and simple sashing – two elements that were also used in the first quilt my grandma and I made together all those years ago. This quilt reminds me of the spaces in a home – rooms, windows, doors, hallways, etc. It's funny how in quilting and life, we return to the same building blocks again and again to create something new – a new house, a new quilt, a new memory.

FIRST BLUSH QUILT 1 // *Materials*

	LIGHT PINK	DARK PINK	BACKING	BINDING
Crib: 27" x 31"	1 yard	¾ yard	1 yard	½ yard (3 strips)
Throw: 54" x 62"	2 ¼ yards	2 yards	3 ½ yards	½ yard (6 strips)
Queen: 81" x 93"	4 yards	3 ½ yards	7 ½ yards	¾ yard (9 strips)

Instructions are written as crib (throw, queen). Queen size variations are marked with an asterisk. Note: This is not a double-sided quilt, but rather two quilt variations. However, you can choose to make it double-sided with the instructions on the following pages.

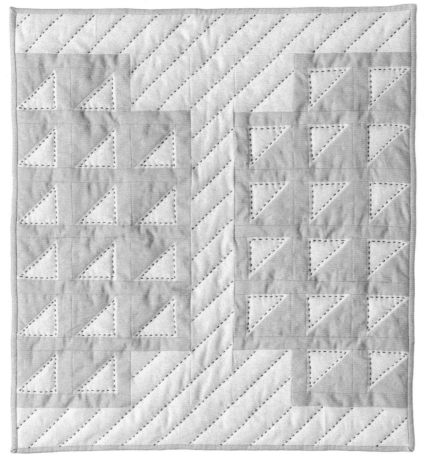

Quilt 1

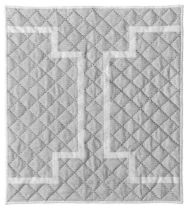

Quilt 2

QUILTING MOTIF // *For Quilt 1, I highlighted the piecing with triangular shapes and simple diagonal quilting lines in the background. I used contrasting brown thread for added interest.*

Cutting Instructions

	LIGHT PINK	DARK PINK
Crib	**(1) 4 ½" x WOF strip, subcut into:** • (4) 4 ½" x 4 ½" (B) **(2) 4" x WOF strips, subcut into:** • (16) 4" x 4" **(3) 3 ½" x WOF strips, subcut into:** • (2) 3 ½" x 27 ½" (A) • (1) 3 ½" x 25 ½" (C)	**(2) 4" x WOF strips, subcut into:** • (16) 4" x 4" **(8) 1 ½" x WOF strips, subcut into:** • (10) 1 ½" x 12 ½" (E) • (4) 1 ½" x 8 ½" (D) • (32) 1 ½" x 3 ½" (F)
Throw	**(1) 8 ½" x WOF strip, subcut into:** • (4) 8 ½" x 8 ½" (B) **(3) 7" x WOF strips, subcut into:** • (16) 7" x 7" **(6) 6 ½" x WOF strips (A & C)**	**(3) 7" x WOF strips, subcut into:** • (16) 7" x 7" **(14) 2 ½" x WOF strips, subcut into:** • (10) 2 ½" x 24 ½ (E) • (4) 2 ½" x 16 ½" (D) • (32) 2 ½" x 6 ½" (F)
Queen	**(2) 12 ½" x WOF strips, subcut into:** • (4) 12 ½" x 12 ½" (B) **(4) 10" x WOF strips, subcut into:** • (16) 10" x 10" **(6) 9 ½" x WOF strips (A & C)**	**(4) 10" x WOF strips, subcut into:** • (16) 10" x 10" **(21) 3 ½" x WOF strips, subcut into:** • (10) 3 ½" x 36 ½" (E) • (4) 3 ½" x 24 ½" (D) • (32) 3 ½" x 9 ½" (F)

Assembly

1. Start by assembling the half-square triangles (HSTs). Take your 4" (7", 10") squares of both colors. Draw a diagonal line on the back of your light-colored squares. Place a light square on top of a dark square, right sides together so the line is facing up toward you. Sew a ¼" seam on either side of the marked line (Diagram 1).

2. Cut on the marked line to form two new squares made of two half-square triangles and press the seams open (Diagram 2). Trim to 3 ½" (6 ½", 9 ½") square. Create 32 HST units.

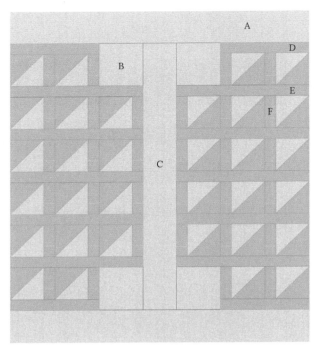

Quilt 1

3. Sew the F rectangles to your new HSTs. Arrange a row of two HSTs and two F rectangles as shown in Diagram 3. Sew all the pieces together, pressing your seams open. Create four of these double-HST units. The double-HST units should measure 3 ½" x 8 ½" (6 ½" x 16 ½", 9 ½" x 24 ½").

4. Sew the D rectangles to the double-HST units from Step 3. Sew two D rectangles to the bottoms of the units, and two D rectangles to the tops of the units (Diagram 4). Set aside until we're ready to assemble the quilt top. The subunits should measure 4 ½" x 8 ½" (8 ½" x 16 ½", 12 ½" x 24 ½").

Diagram 1

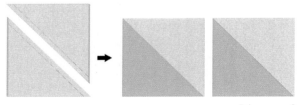

Diagram 2

Diagram 3

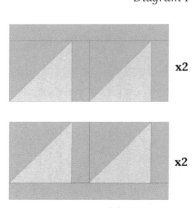

x2

x2

Diagram 4

5. Arrange a row of three HSTs and three F rectangles as shown in Diagram 5. Sew all the pieces together, pressing your seams open. Create eight of these triple-HST units. The triple-HST units should measure 3 ½" x 12 ½" (6 ½" x 24 ½", 9 ½" x 36 ½").

Diagram 5

6. Sew the E rectangles to the triple-HST units from Step 5 to start assembling the focal point of the quilt. Arrange four triple-HST units and five E rectangles as shown in Diagram 6. Sew the rows together and press seams open. Repeat with the remaining four triple-HST units and five E rectangles to create a second column. The column should measure 12 ½" x 17 ½" (24 ½" x 34 ½", 36 ½" x 51 ½").

7. Sew a B square to the double-HST units from Step 4 as shown in Diagram 7. The subunit should measure 4 ½" x 12 ½" (8 ½" x 24 ½", 12 ½" x 36 ½").

8. Assemble one of two focal units by sewing two double-HST units to the top and bottom of a triple-HST unit from Step 6 (Diagram 8). Press seams open and set aside. Repeat to make an identical second focal unit. The focal unit should measure 12 ½" x 25 ½" (24 ½" x 50 ½", 36 ½ x 75 ½").

Diagram 6

TIP FOR LINING UP THE VERTICAL LINES // *Before you pin the rows together, turn the top row down several inches and adjust the layers until the vertical lines (F rectangles) align. Carefully, pin the layers together one seam at a time, starting in the middle and working your way out to each edge.*

x2

x2

Diagram 7

9. For the throw and queen sizes, trim the selvage edges off two C strips. Sew the strips together along the shortest edge. Trim the strip to the average height of the focal units. The throw strip should measure approximately 6 ½" x 50 ½" and the queen strip should measure approximately 9 ½" x 75 ½".

10. Sew your C strip to your two focal units as shown in Diagram 9. Press your seams open. The subunit should measure 27 ½" x 25 ½" (54 ½" x 50 ½", 81 ½" x 75 ½").

11. For the throw and queen sizes, trim the selvage edges off the A strips. Sew two strips together along the shortest edge. Trim the strip to the average width of the subunit from Step 10. The throw strip should measure approximately 6 ½" x 54 ½" and the queen strip should measure approximately 9 ½" x 81 ½". Repeat to make a second strip.

12. Sew the A strips to the top and bottom of your quilt top as shown in Diagram 10. Press your seams open to finish the quilt top. The finished quilt top should measure 27 ½" x 31 ½" (54 ½" x 62 ½", 81 ½" x 93 ½").

Diagram 8

Diagram 9

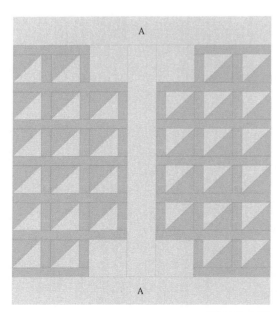

Diagram 10

FIRST BLUSH QUILT 2 // *Materials*

	LIGHT PINK	DARK PINK	BACKING	BINDING
Crib: 27" x 31"	¼ yard	1 yard	1 yard	½ yard (3 strips)
Throw: 54" x 62"	½ yard	3 ½ yards	3 ½ yards	½ yard (6 strips)
Queen: 81" x 93"	1 yard	6 ¾ yards	7 ½ yards	¾ yard (9 strips)

Instructions are written as crib (throw, queen).
Queen size variations are marked with an asterisk.

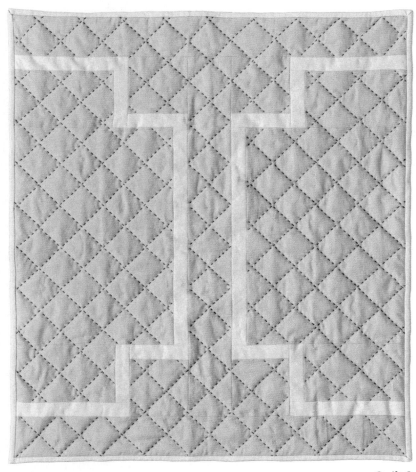

Quilt 2

Quilt 1

QUILTING MOTIF // For

Quilt 2, I decided to quilt a very simple cross-hatch design in the negative space. I like the juxtaposition of the 90° lines in the piecing and the 45° lines in the quilting.

Cutting Instructions

LIGHT PINK	DARK PINK
Crib	
(3) 1 ½" x WOF strips, subcut into: • (2) 1 ½" x 15 ½" (Long strip) • (4) 1 ½" x 8 ½" (Medium strip) • (8) 1 ½" x 4 ½" (Short strip)	**(1) 11 ½" x WOF strip, subcut into:** • (2) 11 ½" x 15 ½"(A) **(2) 4 ½" x WOF strips, subcut into:** • (4) 4 ½" x 7 ½" (B) • (4) 4 ½" x 4 ½" (C) **(3) 3 ½" x WOF strips, subcut into:** • (2) 3 ½" x 27 ½" (E) • (1) 3 ½" x 25 ½" (D)
Throw	
(5) 2 ½" x WOF strips, subcut into: • (2) 2 ½" x 30 ½" (Long strip) • (4) 2 ½" x 16 ½" (Medium strip) • (8) 2 ½" x 8 ½" (Short strip)	**(2) 22 ½" x WOF strips, subcut into:** • (2) 22 ½" x 30 ½"(A) **(3) 8 ½" x WOF strips, subcut into:** • (4) 8 ½" x 14 ½" (B) • (4) 8 ½" x 8 ½" (C) **(6) 6 ½" x WOF strips (D & E)**
Queen	
(8) 3 ½" x WOF strips, subcut into: • (4) 3 ½" x 23" (Long strip) • (4) 3 ½" x 24 ½" (Medium strip) • (8) 3 ½" x 12 ½" (Short strip)	**(2) 45 ½" x WOF strips, subcut into:** • (2) 45 ½" x 33 ½"(A) **(4) 12 ½" x WOF strips, subcut into:** • (4) 12 ½" x 21 ½" (B) • (4) 12 ½" x 12 ½" (C) **(8) 9 ½" x WOF strips (D & E)**

Assembly

1. Sew a long strip* to one side of an A rectangle (Diagram 1). Repeat to make two. Press seams open and set aside. Subunits will be 12 ½" x 15 ½" (24 ½" x 30 ½", 36 ½" x 45 ½").

   *For queen size, sew two 23" strips together end to end to make a 45 ½" long strip. Repeat to sew a second strip.

2. Sew one short strip to the short side of each B rectangle. Repeat to make 4. Press seams open. Subunits should measure 4 ½" x 8 ½" (8 ½" x 16 ½", 12 ½" x 24 ½").

3. Sew one short strip to one side of each C square. Repeat to make four. Press seams open and set aside. Subunits should measure 4 ½" x 5 ½" (8 ½" x 10 ½", 12 ½" x 15 ½").

4. Sew a medium strip to the bottom side of the B subunits from Step 2. Make two pieces where the short strip is on the right, and two where the short strip is on the left (Diagram 2). Press seams open. Subunits should measure 5 ½" x 8 ½" (10 ½" x 16 ½", 15 ½" x 24 ½").

5. Sew the B subunits from Step 4 and C subunits from Step 3 together. Sew the C pieces to the B subunit side with the strip you've already sewn on, making two of each configuration (Diagram 3). Subunits should measure 12 ½" x 5 ½" (24 ½" x 10 ½", 36 ½" x 15 ½").

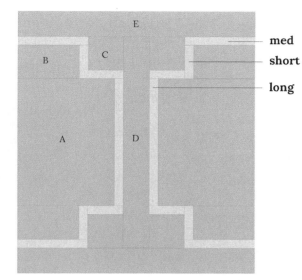

med
short
long

Side 2

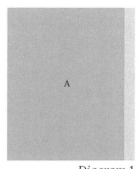

Diagram 1

x2

x2

Diagram 2

x2

x2

Diagram 3

6. Sew two B/C blocks to the top and bottom of one A block as shown in Diagram 4. Press all seams open. Repeat with the other pieces to make a second identical unit. Subunit should measure 12 ½" x 25 ½" (24 ½" x 50 ½", 36 ½" x 75 ½").

7. Take the D rectangle* and arrange it between the two focal pieces as shown in Diagram 5. Sew the three pieces together and press seams open. Subunit should measure 27 ½" x 25 ½" (54 ½" x 50 ½", 81 ½" x 75 ½").

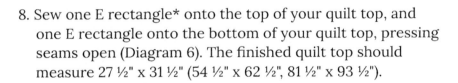

TIP // *For long seams, use pins to hold your pieces in place as you sew. Pin from the outside in to avoid puckers.*

*For throw and queen sizes, remove the selvages from two D WOF strips and sew together end to end to make one long D rectangle. Trim to the average measured height of the subunits from Step 6. The throw size D rectangle should measure approximately 6 ½" x 50 ½" and the queen size D rectangle should measure approximately 9 ½" x 75 ½".

8. Sew one E rectangle* onto the top of your quilt top, and one E rectangle onto the bottom of your quilt top, pressing seams open (Diagram 6). The finished quilt top should measure 27 ½" x 31 ½" (54 ½" x 62 ½", 81 ½" x 93 ½").

*For throw and queen sizes, remove the selvages from two E WOF strips and sew together end to end to make one long E rectangle. Trim to the average width of the subunit from Step 7. Repeat to make two. The throw size E rectangle should measure approximately 6 ½" x 54 ½" and the queen size E rectangle should measure approximately 9 ½" x 81 ½".

Diagram 4

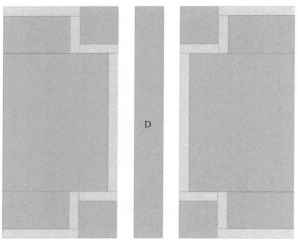

Diagram 5

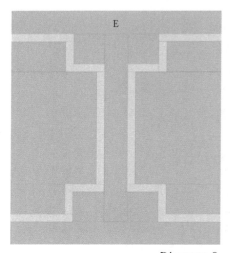

Diagram 6

QUILTS CAN ADD A POP OF COLOR (AND
MOMENTS OF JOY) TO ANY ROOM.

Own

There are only five pieces and four seams that make up Own – but while it looks simple, it may be one of the most challenging quilts in this book to make. The pieces are cut and sewn with unconventional methods, and the quilt relies heavily on quilting lines (however subtle) to create movement. This quilt represents the idea that things are not always as they appear. Just as it's important to pursue new challenges, there is also beauty in nurturing and celebrating simplicity.

OWN SIDE 1 // *Notes*

In this quilt we'll work with bias edges, so there are a few things to consider.

- Try not to handle the fabric too much. Bias edges can be easily warped, so try to handle gently.

- Pin generously and use your walking foot to avoid pulling or stretching.

- Don't be concerned if your seams and edges don't align. That can happen with bias pieces. This quilt can be trimmed, and the finished size is approximate.

- Don't fear the unsquared quilt! The version you see isn't completely square. I left it that way intentionally because I loved how it looked.

This quilt is double-sided, and you can use the Side 2 instructions on page 83 for the back. If you'd rather make a traditional quilt, the backing yardage is indicated in the materials section. Instructions are written twin (crib). Variations are marked with an asterisk.

Note: If making a double-sided quilt, make sure to save all scrap pieces for the back.

Side 1

Side 2

Materials

	WHITE	GRAY	BACKING	BINDING
Crib: 30" x 35"	½ yard	1 ¼ yard	1 yard	½ yard (4 strips)
Twin: 60" x 70"	1 ½ yards	4 yards	3 ¾ yards	¾ yard (7 strips)

Cutting Instructions

	WHITE	GRAY
Crib	**(1) 15 ½" x WOF strip, subcut into:** • (1) 15 ½" x 26 ½" (A)	**(1) 22 ½" x WOF strip, subcut into:** • (1) 22 ½" x 30 ½ (D) **(1) 13 ½" x WOF strip, subcut into:** • (1) 13 ½" x 23 ½" (B) • (1) 13 ½" x 8" (C)
Twin	**(1) 53" x WOF strip, subcut into:** • (1) 53" x 31" (A)	**(1) 45 ½" x WOF strip, subcut into:** • 45 ½" x 26 ½" (B) • 15 ½" x 26 ½" (C) **(2) 44 ½" x WOF strips, subcut into:** • (2) 44 ½ x 30 ½" (D)

TIP FOR CUTTING TWIN RECTANGLE A // *Cut 53" x WOF, then unfold the fabric. Refold the fabric in the opposite direction and line up the cut edges. Pin the cut edges together generously for stability. Trim the selvages from one end. Trim the other end to 31".*

Assembly

1. Arrange the two D rectangles* right sides together. Generously pin one of the long edges. Stitch the pinned edge using a ¼" seam. Press the seam open (Diagram 1). Set these pieces aside for Step 8. Finished subunit should measure 60 ½" x 44 ½".

   This step is not necessary for the crib size.

2. Open the white A rectangle and fold as shown along the diagonal (Diagram 2). Gently press and pin the fold in place generously.

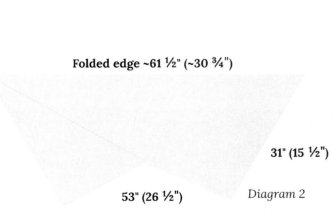

Side 1

3. Cut along the fold using shears to create two triangles that are 53" x 31" x ~61 ½" (15 ½" x 26 ½" x ~30 ¾"). Don't worry if this edge isn't perfectly straight. We will straighten it up later. Unpin and set one triangle aside for Step 6 and set one triangle aside for Side 2.

4. Repeat Steps 2 and 3 using the B rectangle, pinning the fold and cutting on the diagonal in the same way to create two triangles that are 45 ½" x 26 ½" x ~52 ½" (23 ½" x 13 ½" x ~27"). Set one triangle aside for Step 6 and set one triangle aside for the back.

5. Repeat Steps 2 and 3 using the C rectangle, pinning the fold and cutting on the diagonal in the same way to create two triangles that are 26 ½" x 15 ½" x ~30 ¾" (13 ½" x 8" x ~15 ½"). Set one triangle aside for Step 7 and set one triangle aside for Side 2.

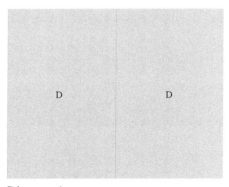

Diagram 1

Folded edge ~61 ½" (~30 ¾")

31" (15 ½")

53" (26 ½")   Diagram 2

6. Arrange one A and one B triangle shown in Diagram 3, right sides together. Center the two pieces so there is an equal amount of overhang at each end — make sure there is more than ¼" of gray fabric that will hang below the white point. This ensures that your point doesn't get buried in the seam. Pin the pieces right sides together generously. Start your stitch at the point shown in Diagram 3 and sew the pieces together using a ¼" seam allowance with the white piece on the bottom. Press your seam open.

Start stitching here

Diagram 3

7. Sew one C triangle the left-hand side of the A triangle in the same way as you sewed the B triangle (Diagram 4). Remember that we will trim later. Pin generously. Start your stitch at the point shown in Diagram 4 and sew the pieces together. Press seam open.

Start stitching here

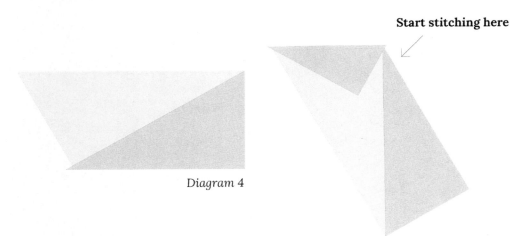

Diagram 4

PRESERVE THE POINT // *You can always trim overhanging fabric, but leave a ¼" seam allowance for yourself underneath the downward-facing point of the A piece. This will help you avoid burying the point in the next step.*

8. Square the edges of your triangle unit (Diagram 5). The triangle subunit should measure approximately 60 ½" x 26 ½" (30 ½" x 13 ½").

SQUARE UP // *Use a tape measure or yard stick to extend the lines of your edges and mark where to trim.*

Diagram 5

9. Pin the triangle subunit from Step 8 to the D rectangle subunit from Step 1, right sides together. Stitch with a ¼" seam. Press your seam open.

10. Trim the top if needed. The final size should be about 60 ½" x 70 ½" (30 ½" x 35 ½").

SQUARING UP YOUR QUILT (OR NOT) //

Your quilt top is done, and you're free to trim if you'd like. You can use the corner of a table or lines in a hardwood floor as guides for squaring up. However, if your quilt isn't straight but you like it that way, great! Some of my favorite quilts are oblong, misshapen or curved around the edges (including the one in this book). Do what feels best to you, and finish the quilt however you like — square or unsquare. Hand quilting will make it even more beautifully imperfect.

Diagram 6

OWN SIDE 2 // *Materials*

	WHITE	GRAY	BACKING	BINDING
Crib: 30" x 35"	1 ¼ yards (only ¾ yard if using scraps from Side 1)	½ yard	1 yard	½ yard (4 strips)
Twin: 60" x 70"	4 yards (only 2 ½ yards if using scraps from Side 1)	1 ½ yards	3 ¾ yards	¾ yard (7 strips)

Instructions are written twin (crib). Variations are marked with an asterisk.

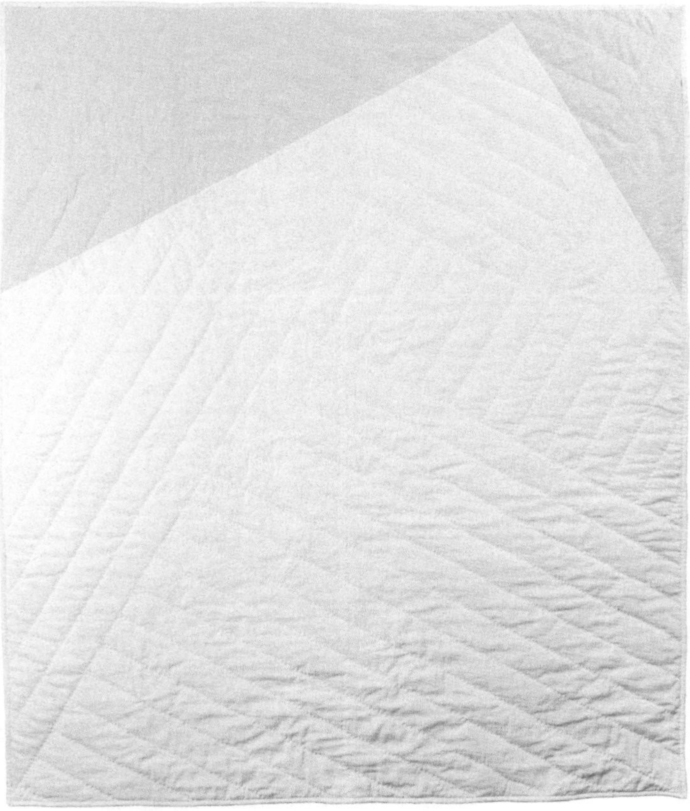

Side 2

Side 1

Cutting Instructions

	WHITE	GRAY
Crib	**(1) 15 ½" x WOF strip, subcut into:** • 15 ½" x 26 ½" (A) * *If you have the other half of your A piece from Side 1, do not cut this.* **(1) 22 ½" x WOF strip, subcut into:** • 22 ½" x 30 ½" (D)	**(1) 13 ½" x WOF strip, subcut into:** • 13 ½" x 23 ½" (B) • 13 ½" x 8" (C)
Twin	**(1) 53" x WOF strip, subcut into:** • (1) 53" x 31" (A) * *If you have the other half of your A piece from Side 1, do not cut this.* **(2) 44 ½" x WOF strips, subcut into:** • (2) 44 ½ x 30 ½" (D)	**(1) 45 ½" x WOF strip, subcut into:** • 45 ½" x 26 ½" (B) • 15 ½" x 26 ½" (C)

TIP FOR CUTTING TWIN RECTANGLE A // *Cut 53" x WOF, then unfold the fabric. Refold the fabric in the opposite direction and line up the cut edges. Pin the cut edges together generously for stability. Trim the selvages from one end. Trim the other end to 31".*

Assembly

1. Using your white D pieces, repeat Step 1 from the Side 1 instructions.

2. Repeat Steps 2–8 in the Side 1 instructions. You will recreate the top triangle portion that we made for the previous side. Square up the triangle portion at the end, but DON'T square up the entire quilt top if you're making this as the backing. If it is the backing, we don't want to trim until after we've basted and we're done quilting.

3. Arrange the fabric pieces as shown in Diagram 7 and pin them together. Stitch together to finish the top!

Side 2

QUILTING MOTIF // *For this quilt, I created a motif that echoes the angles in the piecing but creates a new design in the negative space. I love how the angles that run parallel to the piecing on Side 1 forms the exact opposite angle to the piecing on Side 2 (see the photos on pages 78 and 83). To achieve this look, start at the top of your quilt and draw parallel lines to the seams in piece A. Work your way down the quilt until your lines start to meet each other, then switch directions. You can then use your marked lines as guides to draw perpendicular lines going in the opposite direction. The options are truly endless with this quilt, so make something that is uniquely you! Curves, straight lines and shapes would all look great.*

Diagram 7

THERE ARE FEW RULES TO QUILTMAKING, EXCEPT TO HAVE THREE LAYERS HELD TOGETHER WITH THREAD. EACH QUILT IS AN EXPRESSION OF THE PERSON WHO MADE IT.

COUNTERPART

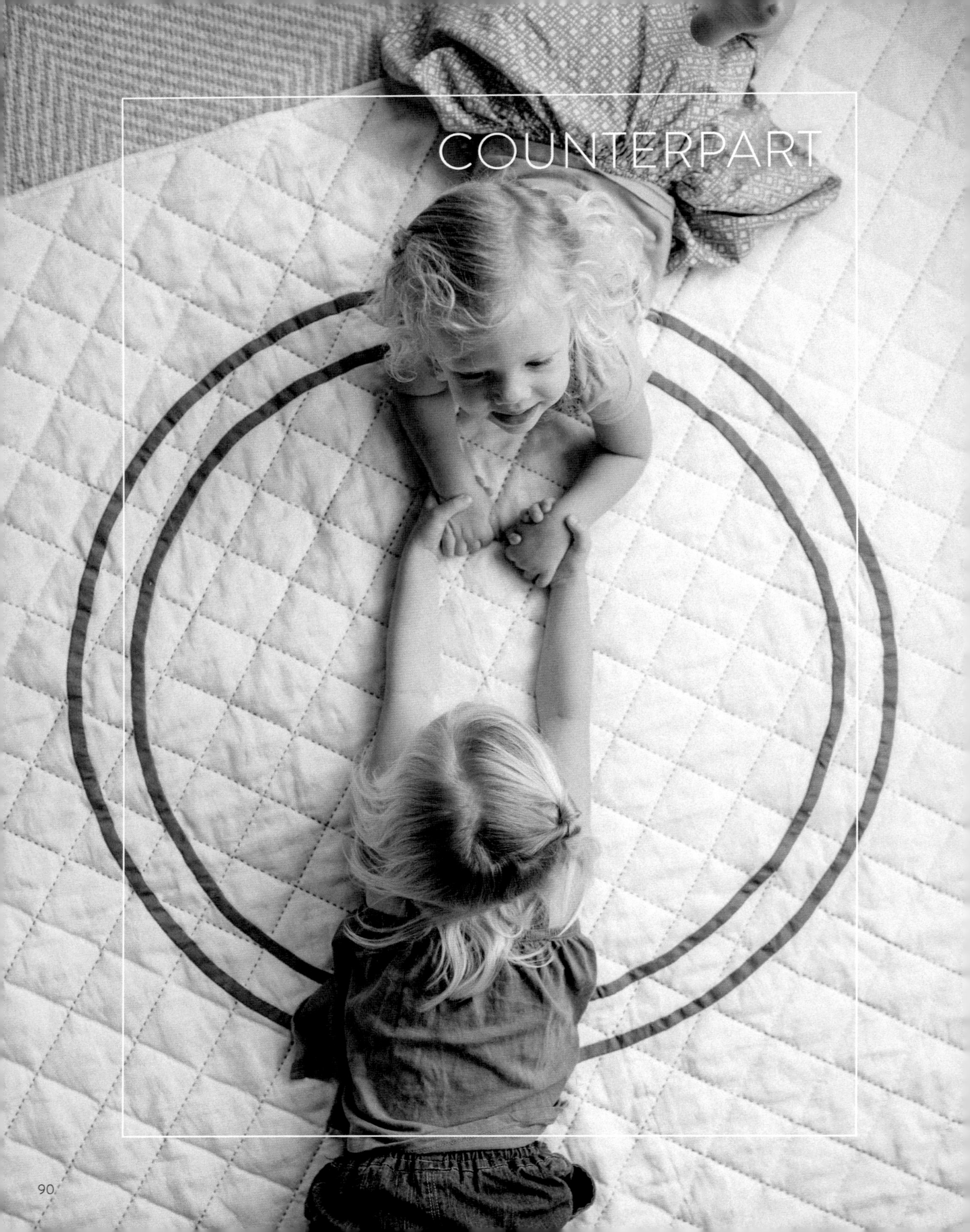

Counterpart

Shortly after my wedding, I wanted to make my own interpretation of a wedding ring quilt, the popular traditional design made for new couples. Though it was originally inspired by wedding bands, the different versions of this quilt now remind me of the many relationships we hold dear — all of our unique counterparts. The quilting lines and arrangement of elements in each quilt intentionally reinforce the harmony, joy, and comfort we experience by moving through life with others.

COUNTERPART QUILT 1 // *Materials*

	WHITE	GRAY	BACKING	BINDING
Throw: 60" x 60"	3 ½ yards	¾ yard	3 ¾ yard	½ yard (6 strips)

Note: This is not a double-sided quilt, but rather two quilt variations. However, you can choose to make it double-sided with the instructions on the following pages.

Cutting Instructions

	WHITE	GRAY
Throw	**(2) 60 ½" x WOF strips, subcut into:** • (2) 60 ½" x 30 ½"	**(1) 18" x WOF strip, subcut into:** • (2) 18" x 18" squares

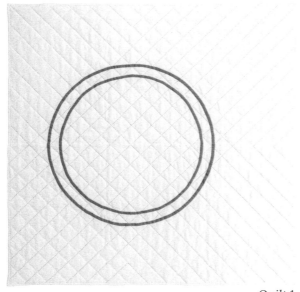

Quilt 1

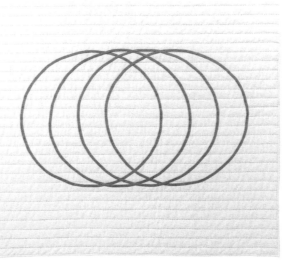

Quilt 2

Assembly

1. Sew your two white rectangles together lengthwise and press open. You should have a 60 ½" x 60 ½" base, onto which we'll appliqué the rings.

2. Make your bias strips. If you have a favorite bias strip method, feel free to make these however you prefer. Otherwise, see the instructions below to make a continuous strip from an 18" x 18" square.

Make Bias Tape Appliqué Strips

- Take your 18" x 18" square and draw a diagonal line from corner to corner. Cut along this line. (Diagram A)

- Layer the two triangle pieces as shown in Diagram B, leaving about ¼" overhang on each side. Sew a ¼" seam across the top. Press your seams open. You should now have a parallelogram shape (Diagram C).

- Cut your parallelogram into 2" strips. Line up your ruler with the longest side of your shape, and start cutting 2" wide strips (Diagram D). If you have any remaining fabric after the last 2" strip, just discard it.

- Align two strips right sides together and overlap the short ends about ¼" to account for the seam allowance (Diagram E). Sew all the strips together and press seams open as you go (Diagram F). You should end up with about 150" of bias tape.

- Once your strip is done, take it to the ironing board and press in half lengthwise so the width is 1" wide, folded. The bias tape strip is now ready to use in your quilt.

Diagram A

Diagram B

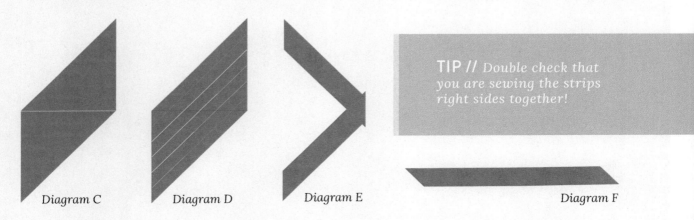

Diagram C

Diagram D

Diagram E

TIP // Double check that you are sewing the strips right sides together!

Diagram F

Marking

3. Press the base to make sure it's wrinkle-free. Measure 26" from the left edge of the base along the center seam (Diagram 1). Make a mark on the seam at the 26" mark. This will be the center of your circle.

4. Take a length of thread or string (at least 18") and tie a knot in one end. You won't be sewing with this, but we will use it to mark our circles. Needle the thread on the other end and insert it through the back of your base at the spot you marked. (Diagram 2)

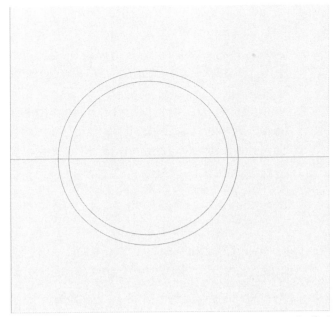

Quilt 1

MARKING // *See the marking workshop on page 96 for detailed instructions.*

5. Leaving your string there, tape your base down to the floor or a large flat surface, as if you were going to baste it. Draw it taut so you can mark a neat, even circle.

6. Next we'll mark the rings, starting with the outer ring. Using a ruler or tape measure, pull the string away from the center and trim it to 17" exactly. Move the string around the quilt in a circle and mark where the string ends, about every 1" or so. Continue until you have a full circle. Go back and connect the dots to make a marked circle with a 34" diameter (Diagram 3).

7. Next, measure your string again and trim it to 15" long from the center. Mark the quilt top in the same way as in the last step, this time making a circle that is 30" in diameter (Diagram 4).

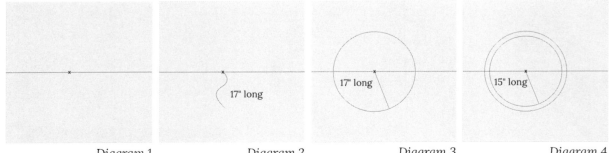

| Diagram 1 | Diagram 2 | Diagram 3 | Diagram 4 |

Appliqué

8. Lay one of your bias strips down so the folded edge matches up with the inner marked line (the raw edges should face inward). Use safety pins to pin it in place. Repeat with the other bias strip, pinning so the folded edge matches up with the outer ring.

9. Now it's time to start appliquéing. You'll start with the folded edge for the inside ring. Use an invisible stitch (like you would for binding), and sew the folded edge of the bias strip along the marked line.

Diagram 5

When it's time to join the two ends of your bias strip, pin them down along the marked line so they overlap. Trim the tails so they overlap by exactly ¼". Take your quilt to the sewing machine and turn the bias strip tails right sides together. Pin, if desired, and stitch a straight seam to join them (Diagram 5). Press seams open, and re-press the fold. The bias strip should now be the perfect length for your marked line, but keep in mind that the bias strip will stretch, so you have some wiggle room. Continue appliquéing the folded edge until the entire ring is stitched down. Repeat Step 9 for the outer ring.

10. To stitch the raw edges, start with the inner ring and fold the raw edges completely under the bias strip so the width of your finished bias strip ring is ½". Pin if desired, and snip any rogue tails as needed to reduce bulk. Stitch the edge down, turning under as you move around the ring. Repeat with the outer ring to finish the top (Diagram 6).

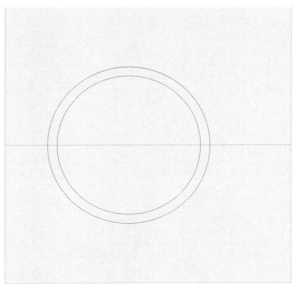

APPLIQUÉ // *Refer to pg. 22 for instructions on how to appliqué.*

Diagram 6

Counterpart Marking Workshop

The best way to appliqué smooth and tidy circles is to mark them accurately. This is my method for marking large circles. Make sure to use a non-stretchy string for best results.

Thread a piece of string and insert through the back of your top at the marked center point of your circle. Make sure you have a ruler, some snips and a pencil with an eraser nearby.

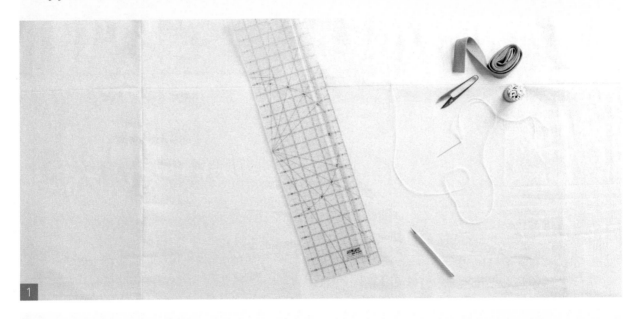

Measure the string from the center point and snip to the length indicated.

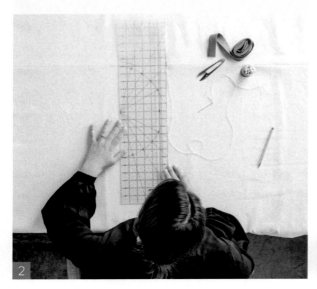

Pull the string tight and draw hash marks on the fabric where the string ends.

Continue making hash marks every ½"–1" around the entire circle.

Reposition the string and the pencil to make each mark.

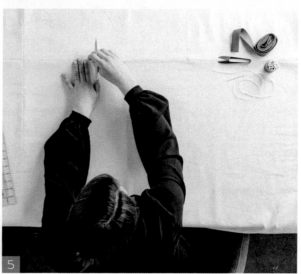

MARKING IS THE KEY TO SUCCESS IN THIS QUILT. THE CLEANER YOUR LINES, THE SMOOTHER THE FINISHED CIRCLES WILL BE.

When you're done, go back and fill in the line of your circle. You can use the eraser to erase and redraw lines as needed.

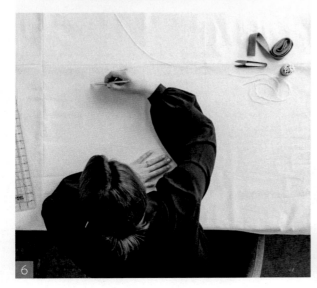

Carefully mark the rest of the circle until you have a smooth, continuous line.

COUNTERPART QUILT 2 // *Materials*

	WHITE	GRAY	BACKING	BINDING
Throw: 60" x 60"	3 ½ yards	1 ½ yards	3 ¾ yard	½ yard (6 strips)

Cutting Instructions

	WHITE	GRAY
Throw	**(2) 60 ½" x WOF strips, subcut into:** • (2) 60 ½" x 30 ½"	**(2) 18" x WOF strips, subcut into:** • (4) 18" x 18" squares *

*You will have enough fabric if you make only three squares' worth of bias strips, but you'll have to join the leftovers together after you complete the first three appliqué circles (step 6).

1. Follow Steps 1–2 from Side 1 and make your bias strips (pg. 93).

2. Press your base fabric and make sure it is free of wrinkles. Measure 21" in from the left edge of the base, along the center seam (Diagram 1). Make a mark on the seam at the following intervals:

   • 21" – Circle A
   • 27" – Circle B
   • 33" – Circle C
   • 39" – Circle D

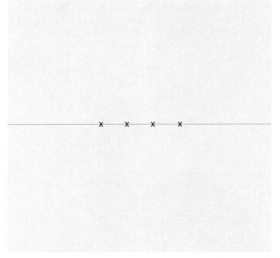

Diagram 1

3. Follow Steps 4-10 from Side 1, but use four lengths of thread (one for each point you marked on the front). Insert all the thread through the back before you tape your quilt to the ground. You'll use one 15" length of string at each marked location to measure each circle (but trim to 15" after your quilt is taped down). Draw your circles (Diagram 2). Refer to page 96 for detailed instructions.

4. Appliqué your bias strips down using the methods from the previous side (page 95). Make sure your bias strip tapes are arranged so the folded edge matches up with the marked line (the raw edges should face inward). Use safety pins to pin in place if desired. Work outside to inside, so appliqué the circles in this order: A, D, B, C (Diagram 3 – colors are for emphasis only).

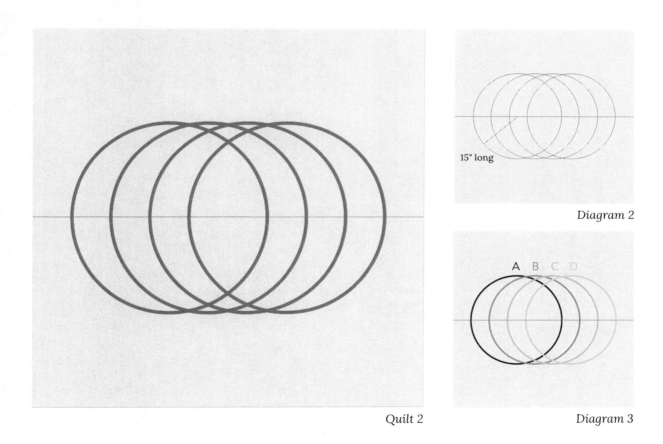

15" long

Diagram 2

Quilt 2

A B C D

Diagram 3

OVERLAPPING RINGS // *Use the intersections of the rings as guidelines to create smooth curves as you're appliquéing. Try to evenly space the gaps at the top and bottom of the rings, and try to make the edges of the rings lie on the same plane. You can mark a horizontal line on the background to help with this.*

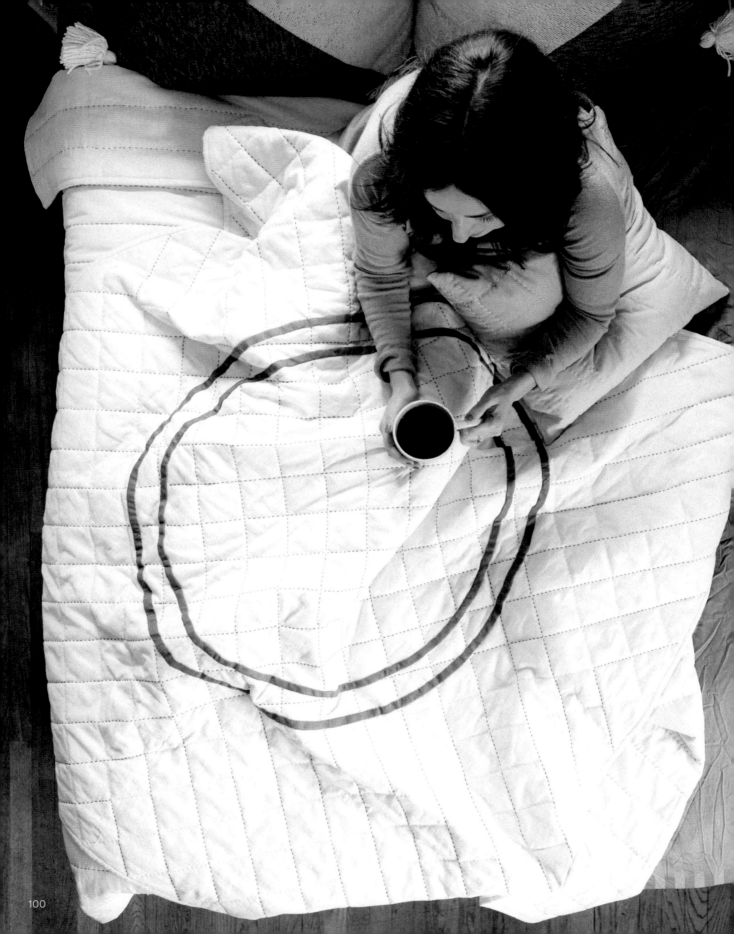

MODERN HEIRLOOMS ARE
BEAUTIFUL, FUNCTIONAL AND
LASTING. A WELL CRAFTED QUILT
CAN LAST A LIFETIME.

PRINCE

Prince

This quilt is inspired by a crown. It's a reminder to be confident, live the life you want, try something new, and practice until you get good at it – lessons that were instilled in me by my parents, grandparents, and so many amazing role models throughout life. This quilt is best for the confident beginner or intermediate quilter, but after making width-of-fabric half-rectangle triangles, you might just feel like you can rule the world.

PRINCE SIDE 1 // *Materials*

	YELLOW	WHITE	BACKING	BINDING
Crib: 31 ½" x 43"	¾ yard	1 ¾ yards	1 ½ yards	½ yard (4 strips)
Twin: 63" x 83"	1 ¼ yards	4 ¾ yards	5 ¼ yards	¾ yard (8 strips)

This quilt is double-sided, and you can use the Side 2 instructions on page 111 for the back. If you'd rather make a traditional quilt, the backing yardage is indicated above. Instructions are written twin (crib). Variations are marked with an asterisk. WOF is assumed to be 43".

Side 1

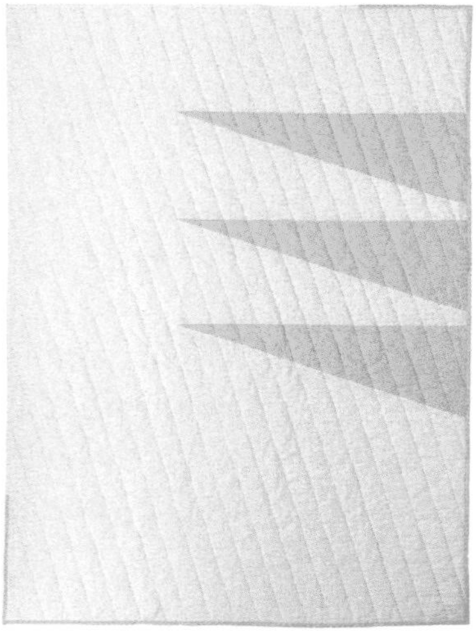

Side 2

QUILTING MOTIF // *The quilting motif accentuates the piecing by following the same angles. The two-tone binding frames the quilt and adds a pop of interest.*

Cutting Instructions

	YELLOW	WHITE
Crib	**(3) 7" x WOF strips (A)** • *You will use these pieces for the triangles on the back as well. If making a single-sided quilt, only cut two WOF strips.*	**(1) 17" x WOF strip (E)** **(1) 7 ½" x WOF strip (B)** **(4) 7" x WOF strips, subcut into:** • *Set aside (3) 7" x WOF strips (A)* • *You will use these pieces for the triangles on the back as well. If making a single-sided quilt, only cut three WOF strips and set aside two for (A).* • *Set aside (1) 7" x WOF strip (C)* **(1) 5 ½" x WOF strip (D)**
Twin	**(3) 14" x WOF strips (A)** • *You will use these pieces for the triangles on the back as well. If making a single-sided quilt, only cut two WOF strips.*	**(2) 30 ½" x WOF strips (E)** **(1) 14 ½" x WOF strip (B)** **(3) 14" x WOF strips (A)** • *You will use these pieces for the triangles on the back as well. If making a single-sided quilt, only cut two WOF strips.* **(2) 13 ½" x WOF strips (C)** **(1) 10 ½" x WOF strip (D)**

BIAS SEAMS // *The half-rectangle triangles in this quilt have a long bias seam down their centers. Handle gently, pin generously, and avoid stretching and pulling for best results.*

Assembly

1. Stack three white and three yellow A WOF strips on top of each other. Trim the selvages and make the A rectangles 43" (21 ½") in length.

NOTE // *It's okay to include a small bit of selvage here (about ½" on either side of the rectangle). We will trim later, so this will not impact the design or construction of the quilt.*

2. Use a long ruler or a tape measure to mark a diagonal line from one corner of the rectangles to the other. Cut along these lines so you have six white triangles and six yellow triangles.

3. Pair one white triangle unit to its complementary yellow triangle unit (this should be the piece on the opposite side of the cut – not the piece stacked above or below). Make sure the yellow triangle points up toward the right (Diagram 1). Stack the two triangle units right sides together, centered over each other and offset by ½" (Diagram 2). Pin generously and sew on the diagonal to make a half-rectangle triangle (HRT) (Diagram 3).

TIP // *Don't handle the pieces too much and try not to stretch them. This is a long bias edge, and it will stretch and warp easily without careful handling.*

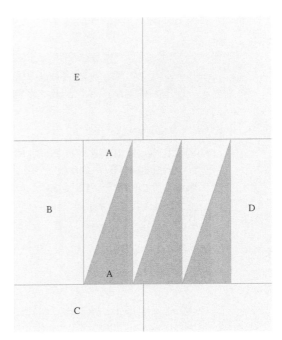

Side 1

TIP // *Don't have a long ruler? Ask a friend to hold your tape measure taut from corner to corner, or use painters tape. Also, make sure the top edge of your fabric is straight with a line on the cutting mat to get an accurate cut.*

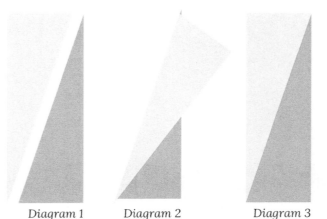

Diagram 1   Diagram 2   Diagram 3

4. Trim the width to 13 ½" (7"), making sure to trim an equal amount from each side. Trim about ½" from each side so the length is 40 ½" (20 ½").

Diagram 4

5. Repeat with the other pieces to make a total of six HRT units. Set aside three HRT units for Side 2.

6. Arrange the HRTs as shown in Diagram 5, and sew them together. Press your seams open. Trim any edges as needed. Subunit should measure 39 ½" x 40 ½" (20" x 20 ½").

TIP // *To get perfect points, make sure there is ¼" space between the diagonal seam and the edge of the piece (Diagram 4).*

TIP // *Every machine and every ¼" seam is a little different, so don't worry if you don't get perfect points right away! Experiment with your seam allowance to see what works for you. On my machine, I find I need to sew just wider than ¼" to get the best points on my HRTs.*

Diagram 5

7. Trim the selvages off the D WOF strip and trim to the average height of the subunit from Step 7, approximately 40 ½" (20 ½"). Sew the D rectangle to the right side of your HRT unit as shown in Diagram 6. Press your seams open. Subunit should measure 49 ½" x 40 ½" (25" x 20 ½").

Diagram 6

8. Trim the selvages off the B WOF strip and trim to the average height of the subunit from Step 8, approximately 40 ½" (20 ½"). Sew the B rectangle to the left side of your HRT unit as shown in Diagram 7. Press your seams open. Subunit should measure 63 ½" x 40 ½" (32" x 20 ½").

Diagram 7

10. Cut the selvages off the C WOF strips and sew them together end to end so you have a piece that is 13 ½" wide and very long*. Trim to the average width of the subunit from Step 9, approximately 13 ½" x 63 ½" (7" x 32"). Line up this piece along the bottom side of your HRT and sew it on to create the bottom border. Press your seam open. (Diagram 8) Subunit should measure 63 ½" x 53 ½" (32" x 27").

For the crib size, you already have a single C piece and do not need to sew two pieces together.

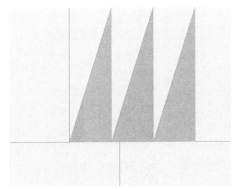

Diagram 8

TIP // *You can measure and trim to center the twin size C rectangle center seam with the HRT unit, but it's not necessary since the quilt top is asymmetrical anyway. There's no shame in saving fabric!*

11. Cut the selvages off the E WOF strips and sew them along the 30 ½" side so the finished strip is 30 ½" tall and over 80" wide*. Trim to the average width of the subunit from Step 10, approximately 30 ½" x 63 ½" (17" x 32"). Attach this border to the top of your HRT unit in the same way as in the previous step. Press seam open (Diagram 9). The pieced quilt top should measure 63 ½" x 83 ½" (32" x 43 ½").

For the crib size, you already have a single E piece and do not need to sew two pieces together.

ADAPTING THE PATTERN //
Because this quilt so much negative space, you can easily adapt it to suit your style. Make it bigger, smaller, or experiment with color.

Diagram 9

PRINCE SIDE 2 // *Materials*

	YELLOW	WHITE	BACKING	BINDING
Crib: 31 ½" x 43"	½ yard	1 ½ yards	1 ½ yards	½ yard (4 strips)
Twin: 63" x 83"	1 yard	2 ¾ yard	5 ¼ yards	¾ yard (8 strips)

This quilt is double-sided, and you can use the Side 1 instructions on page 106 for the back. If you'd rather make a traditional quilt, the backing yardage is indicated in the materials section.

Instructions are written twin (crib). Variations are marked with an asterisk. WOF is assumed to be 43".

Side 2

Side 1

ON THE BACK // *If you're making a double-sided quilt, don't be afraid to leave the backside larger and trim later.*

Cutting Instructions

	YELLOW	WHITE
Crib	**(2) 7" x WOF strips (A)** • Cut ONLY if you didn't make additional HRTs on Side 1	**(1) 22" x WOF strip, subcut into:** • (2) 12" x 22" (D) **(1) 15" x WOF strip, subcut into:** • (1) 15" x 20 ½" (C) **(1) 7 ½" x WOF strip, subcut into:** • (1) 7 ½" x 20 ½" (B) **(1) 1 ½" x WOF strip, subcut into:** • (2) 1 ½" x 20 ½" (E)
Twin	**(2) 14" x WOF strips (A)** • Cut ONLY if you didn't make additional HRTs on Side 1	**(1) 28" x WOF strip, subcut into:** • (1) 28" x 40 ½" (C) **(2) 23 ½" x WOF strips (D)** **(1) 13" x WOF strip, subcut into:** • (1) 13" x 40 ½" (B) **(2) 2 ½" x WOF strips, subcut into:** • (2) 2 ½" x 40 ½" (E)

USE THE LEFTOVERS // *If you made half-rectangle triangles for the front already, you don't need to make more. Have leftovers? Use them for a pillow or another sewing project!*

Assembly

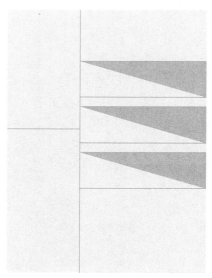

1. Gather the three HRT units leftover from the front side of the quilt (or make three new ones following Steps 1–4 from Side 1).

2. Sew an E rectangle to the top of two of the HRT units as shown in Diagram 10. Press seams open. Sew the two HRT units together with the third HRT unit. Subunit should measure 40 ½" x 43 ½" (20 ½" x 22").

3. Sew the B rectangle to the top of your HRT unit as shown in Diagram 11. Press seam open. Subunit should measure 40 ½" x 56" (20 ½" x 29").

Side 2

4. Sew the C rectangle to the bottom of your HRT unit as shown in Diagram 12. Press seam open. Subunit should measure 40 ½" x 83 ½" (20 ½" x 43 ½")

5. Trim the selvages from the D WOF strips and sew the D rectangles together along the short edges so you have a strip that is 23 ½" wide (12" wide) and over 80" long (43 ½" long). Trim to the average measured height of the subunit from Step 4, approximately 23 ½" x 83 ½" (12" x 43 ½"). Sew this to the left side of your HRT unit as shown in Diagram 13 to attach the final border. Trim the excess fabric away to finish the top! Quilt top should measure 63 ½" x 83 ½" (32" x 43 ½").

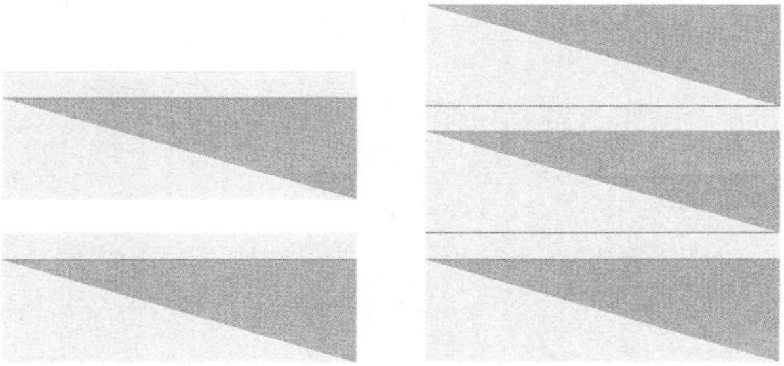

Diagram 10

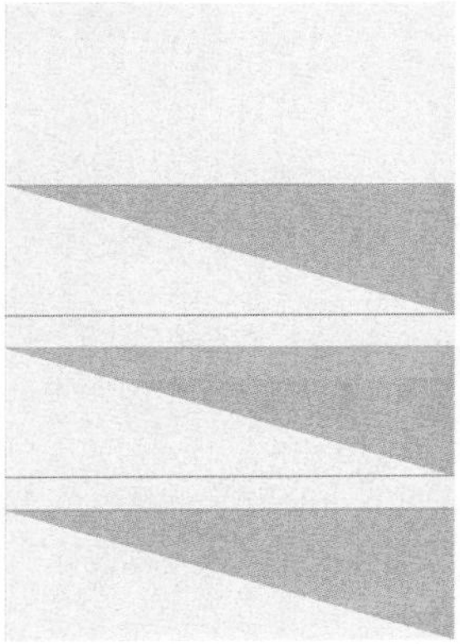

Diagram 11

Diagram 12

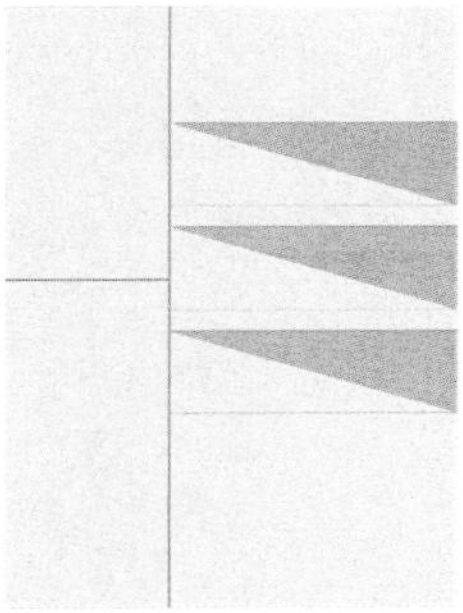

Diagram 13

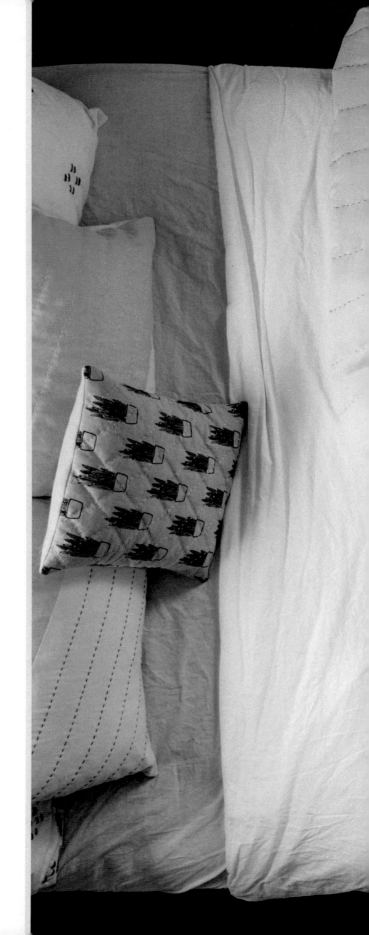

I REMEMBER SLEEPING UNDER HANDMADE QUILTS EVERY TIME I VISITED MY GRANDMOTHER'S HOUSE. SHE ALWAYS MADE THEM TO BE USED AND ENJOYED.

COMPANION

Companion

This quilt was inspired by my dog, Dallas. He is my constant companion and the best studio dog. He also uses the quilts more than anyone (naps are very important). Dallas is a black lab, and this design was my interpretation of what he looks like laying on a quilt – a big, fuzzy ball of love. This quilt is the perfect size for an office or studio, and is a go-anywhere, ready-for-anything kind of quilt, just like Dal.

COMPANION SIDE 1 // *Materials*

	WHITE	BLACK	BACKING	BINDING
Throw: 42" x 42"	1 yard	¾ yard	2 ⅔ yards	½ yard (5 strips)

This quilt is double-sided, and you can use the Side 2 instructions on page 122 for the back. If you'd rather make a traditional quilt, the backing yardage is indicated above.

Cutting Instructions

	WHITE	BLACK
Throw	**(1) 32" x WOF strip**	**(1) 24" x WOF strip**

Side 1

Side 2

QUILTING MOTIF //
The quilting lines simply run perpendicular to the seam to compliment the design.

Assembly

1. Lay the two pieces on top of each other and align the selvages. Trim the selvages off so your two pieces are both the same size (42–43" wide).

2. Lay your white rectangle right side up horizontally on your workspace. Make a mark 19" down from the top right corner. Draw a line from your mark to the bottom left corner (Diagram 1). Cut along the line. Discard the small triangle, or save it for a future project. Set your white piece aside.

3. Lay your black rectangle right side up horizontally on your workspace. Make a mark 11" up from the bottom left corner. Draw a line from your mark to the upper right corner (Diagram 2). Cut along the line. Discard the small triangle, or save it for a future project.

4. Arrange your pieces so the angles align. Flip them right sides together along the angled edges (Diagram 3). Overlap the edges by about ½", and pin in place. Sew the pieces together and press your seam open. Trim your edges square to finish.

Side 1

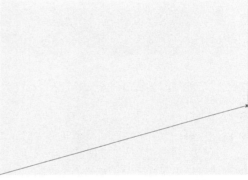

Diagram 1

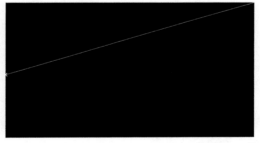

Diagram 2

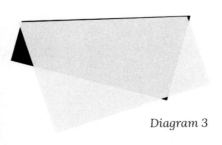

Diagram 3

COMPANION SIDE 2 // *Materials*

	WHITE	BLACK	BACKING	BINDING
Throw: 42" x 42"	1 yard	¾ yard	2 ⅔ yards	½ yard (5 strips)

The back is a mirror image of the front. When basted together, the color blocks will match up as shown below. If you'd like to make a traditional backing, the yardage is indicated above.

Cutting Instructions

	WHITE	BLACK
Throw	**(1) 32" x WOF strip**	**(1) 24" x WOF strip**

Side 2

Side 1

Assembly

1. Lay the two pieces on top of each other and align the selvages. Trim the selvages off so your two pieces are both the same size (42-43" wide).

2. Lay your white rectangle right side up horizontally on your workspace. Make a mark 19" down from the top left corner. Draw a line from your mark to the bottom right corner (Diagram 4). Cut along the line. Discard the small triangle, or save it for a future project. Set your white piece aside.

3. Lay your black rectangle right side up horizontally on your workspace. Make a mark 11" up from the bottom right corner. Draw a line from your mark to the upper left corner (Diagram 5). Cut along the line. Discard the small triangle, or save it for a future project.

4. Arrange your pieces so the angles align. Flip them right sides together along the angled edges (Diagram 6). Overlap the edges by about ½", and pin in place. Sew the pieces together and press your seam open. Trim the edges square to finish.

Side 2

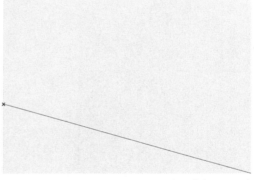

Diagram 4

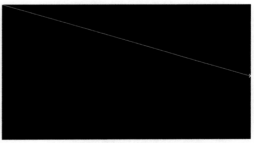

Diagram 5

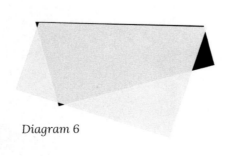

Diagram 6

*QUILTS WITH SIMPLE PIECING ARE EASY
TO CUSTOMIZE TO YOUR HOME AND STYLE.
CHOOSE FABRICS AND COLORS THAT SPEAK
TO YOU, AND MAKE SOMETHING THAT
IS TRULY PERSONAL.*

GUEST
PILLOW

Guest Pillow

The Guest Pillow was inspired by the same design as Companion, but on a smaller scale. This pillow is simple to sew and fat-quarter friendly, so you can make as many as you want. Just like house guests, these pillows can always cheer me up and make the house feel a little brighter.

GUEST PILLOW // *Materials*

DARK	LIGHT	BACKING	CLOSURES	BATTING
Fat quarter or at least 11" x 15"	Fat quarter or at least 11" x 15"	Fat quarter or at least 16" x 16"	(2) fat quarters, or (2) pieces at least 12" x 14 ½"	15 ½" x 15 ½" piece

The finished size of this pillow is 14 ½" x 14 ½", which will fit a 14" x 14" pillow insert.

Cutting Instructions

DARK	LIGHT	CLOSURES
(1) 11" x 15"	**(1) 11" x 15"**	**(2) 12" x 14 ½"**

Assembly

1. Place the light rectangle on top of the dark rectangle right sides facing up so all four edges align. On the light piece, mark a spot 5" up from the bottom right corner (Diagram 1).

2. Cut the fabric from the bottom left corner to the spot you marked to form two angled pieces (Diagram 2).

3. Flip the pieces around so they form a square (Diagram 3). Turn the pieces right sides together and pin in place.

TIP // *Overlap the pieces just slightly so your ¼" seam will start at the place where the dark and light fabrics meet. This helps avoid overhanging edges when you stitch the pieces together.*

4. Stitch the dark and light pieces together along the angled lines (Diagram 4). Press seam open and trim to 15" square to finish (don't worry if it is not quite 15" square; we will trim again after quilting).

NO PRESSURE // *Pillows are very forgiving. If your pillow isn't quite 15" square at this stage, don't worry! You can always trim later and adjust for the final pillow.*

Diagram 1

Diagram 2

Diagram 3

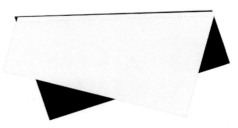

Diagram 4

Quilt

5. Mark your desired quilting marks on the pillow top, using chalk or a pencil. Make your quilt sandwich by basting the backing, batting and pillow top together with pins. Quilt as desired. Remove pins and trim pillow top to 14 ½" square.

Make the Envelope Backing

6. Take your two 12" x 14 ½" rectangles, which will be our envelope closures. Hem one long side of each: Turn the edge under ¼", press, then turn it under another ¼" and press again. Topstitch the hem down, close to the edge (Diagram 5). Double stitch for extra stability. Repeat with the other envelope closure piece.

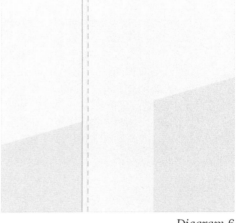

Diagram 5

7. Lay the envelope closure pieces on top of your finished pillow top, with the finished side down. The envelope pieces should overlap by about 4" (Diagram 6).

8. Top stitch around the edges of the pillow top, backstitching at the end to secure (Diagram 7).

Diagram 6

9. Trim the corners to reduce bulk, then turn the pillow right side out. Press to remove any wrinkles, and insert your pillow form.

CHOOSING AN INSERT // *Pillow inserts come in a variety of materials and price points. For a firm pillow, try a cotton or polyester insert. For a slouchy pillow, opt for a down or down-alternative insert. You decide what works best for you!*

Diagram 7

PRACTICE YOUR DESIGN SKILLS BY SCALING OR ALTERING THE PATTERN TO CREATE PILLOWS OF DIFFERENT SHAPES AND SIZES.

HEARTH

Hearth

With Hearth, I was inspired to make a minimalist log cabin block – one of my favorite traditional quilt designs. I decided to call it hearth after an evening spent with my sister and our husbands. We lit a fire in her wood-burning fireplace and talked for hours, just enjoying each others' company. By the end of the evening, the quilt smelled faintly of smoke, and we parted ways, grateful for time spent together. As she was designing this book, my sister told me this was one of her favorite quilts.

HEARTH SIDE 1 // *Materials*

	WHITE	PINK	BACKING	BINDING
Throw: 40" x 45"	1 ¼ yards	1 ¼ yards	2 ¾ yards	½ yard (5 strips)
Twin: 60 ½" x 67 ½"	2 yards	2 ¾ yards	4 yards	¾ yard (7 strips)
Queen: 80" x 90"	3 yards	3 ½ yards	7 ¼ yards	¾ yard (9 strips)

This quilt is double-sided, and you can use the Side 2 instructions on page 142 for the other side. If you'd rather make a traditional quilt, the backing yardage is indicated above.

Instructions are written throw (twin, queen). Variations are marked with an asterisk.

Side 2

Side 1

QUILTING MOTIF // *I used a simple diagonal motif for this quilt to let the piecing stand on its own. I switched thread colors in the different fabrics to add an extra, subtle design element.*

Cutting Instructions

WHITE	PINK
Throw	
(1) 20 ½" x WOF strip, subcut into: • (1) 20 ½" x 25 ½" (A) **(2) 5 ½" x WOF strips, subcut into:** • (2) 5 ½" x 30 ½" (C)	**(6) 5 ½" x WOF strips, subcut into:** • (2) 5 ½" x 40 ½" (E) • (2) 5 ½" x 35 ½" (D) • (1) 5 ½" x 30 ½" (C) • (2) 5 ½" x 20 ½" (B)
Twin	
(1) 30 ½" x WOF strip, subcut into: • (1) 30 ½" x 38" (A) **(4) 8" x WOF strips, subcut into:** • (4) 8" x 23" (C)	**(11) 8" x WOF strips, subcut into:** • (4) 8" x 30 ½" (E) • (1) 8" x 30 ½" (B) • (4) 8" x 26 ¾" (D) • (2) 8" x 23" (C)
Queen	
(1) 50 ½" x WOF strip, subcut into: • (1) 50 ½" x 40 ½" (A) **(4) 10 ½" x WOF strips, subcut into:** • (4) 10 ½" x 30 ½" (C)	**(11) 10 ½" x WOF strips, subcut into:** • (1) 10 ½" x 40 ½" (B) • (2) 10 ½" x 30 ½" (C) • Reserve remaining (8) strips (D & E)

CUT, PIECE, TRIM // *Alternatively, you can cut all the WOF strips and leave them as is, then trim to size as you piece each section. This makes the top even quicker to sew.*

Assembly

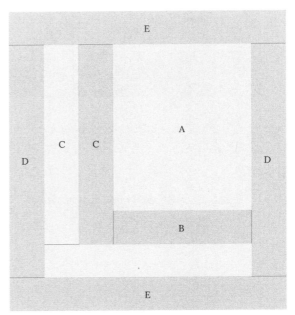

Side 1

1. Sew the white A rectangle and the pink B rectangle together as shown in Diagram 1. Press seam open. This is the beginning of your center unit. Subunit should measure 20 ½" x 30 ½" (30 ½" x 45 ½", 40 ½" x 60 ½").

2. Sew the pink C rectangle* to the left side of your center unit (Diagram 2). Press seam open. Subunit should measure 25 ½" x 30 ½" (38" x 45 ½", 50 ½" x 60 ½").

   *Prior to sewing the twin and queen pink C rectangle to the left, first sew the two C rectangles together along the short edges to create a rectangle that is 8" x 45 ½" (10 ½" x 60 ½").

3. Take your two white C rectangles*. Sew one to the left side of your center unit and press seam open. Subunit should measure 30 ½" x 30 ½" (45 ½" x 45 ½", 60 ½" x 60 ½"). Sew the other white C rectangle* to the bottom of your center unit and press seam open (Diagram 3). Subunit should measure 30 ½" x 35 ½" (45 ½" x 53", 60 ½" x 70 ½").

   *Prior to sewing the twin and queen white C rectangle to the left or bottom, first sew two C rectangles together along the short edges to create a rectangle that is 8" x 45 ½" (10 ½" x 60 ½").

Diagram 1

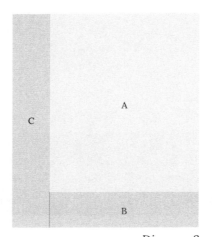

Diagram 2

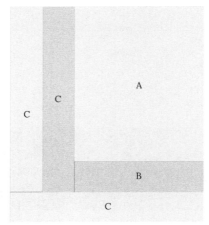

Diagram 3

4. Take your two pink D rectangles*
   and sew them to the left and right
   of your center unit (Diagram 4).
   Press seams open. Subunit
   should measure 40 ½" x 35 ½"
   (60 ½" x 53", 80 ½" x 70 ½").

   *Prior to sewing the twin and queen
   pink D rectangle to the left or right, first
   trim selvage edges from WOF strips and
   sew two D rectangles together along the
   short edges. Trim as necessary to create a
   rectangle that is 8" x 53" (10 ½" x 70 ½").

5. Take your two pink E rectangles*
   and sew them to the top and
   bottom of your center unit
   (Diagram 5). Press seams open to
   finish the top. Finished quilt top
   should measure 40 ½" x 45 ½"
   (60 ½" x 68", 80 ½" x 90 ½").

   *Prior to sewing the twin and queen pink
   E rectangles to the top or bottom, first
   trim selvage edges from WOF strips and
   sew two E rectangles together along the
   short edges. Trim as necessary to create a
   rectangle that is 8" x 60 ½" (10 ½" x 80 ½").

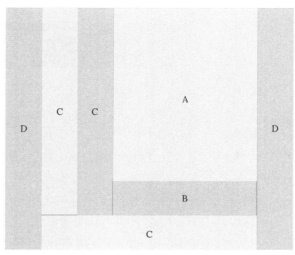

Diagram 4

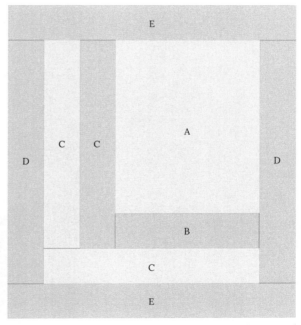

Diagram 5

SQUARE EDGES // *I like to use
the corner of my sewing table to trim my
corners. You can also use painters tape on
the floor or a large, square ruler.*

A QUICK FINISH // *You'll be surprised at how quick this quilt sews up at any size. It
makes a great gift and can be sewn in a variety of colors, perfect for customizing to family and
friends. Making a double-sided quilt? Try a coordinating-but-different color palette on the back
for a little extra drama (and to make it even more fun as a reversible quilt).*

HEARTH SIDE 2 // *Materials*

	WHITE	PINK	BACKING	BINDING
Throw: 40" x 45"	1 ½ yards	1 yard	2 ¾ yards	½ yard (5 strips)
Twin: 60 ½" x 67 ½"	3 yards	1 ¾ yards	4 yards	¾ yard (7 strips)
Queen: 80" x 90"	4 ½ yards	2 ½ yards	7 ¼ yards	¾ yard (9 strips)

This quilt is double-sided, and you can use the Side 1 instructions on page 138 for the other side. If you'd rather make a traditional quilt, the backing yardage is indicated above. Instructions are written throw (twin, queen). Variations are marked with an asterisk.

Side 2

Side 1

QUILTING MOTIF // *I love how the diagonal quilting continues on Side 2 in the opposite direction (toward the open section). Think about how your quilting will translate on the back when marking.*

Cutting Instructions

WHITE	PINK
Throw	
(1) 20 ½" x WOF strip, subcut into: • (1) 20 ½" x 25 ½" (A) **(4) 5 ½" x WOF strips, subcut into:** • (2) 5 ½" x 40 ½" (E) • (2) 5 ½" x 35 ½" (D) • (1) 5 ½" x 5 ½"	**(4) 5 ½" x WOF strips, subcut into:** • (2) 5 ½" x 30 ½" (C) • (1) 5 ½" x 25 ½" (F) • (1) 5 ½" x 20 ½" (B)
Twin	
(1) 30 ½" x WOF strip, subcut into: • (1) 30 ½" x 38" (A) **(8) 8" x WOF strips, subcut into:** • (4) 8" x 30 ½" (E) • (4) 8" x 26 ¾" (D) • (1) 8" x 8"	**(6) 8" x WOF strips, subcut into:** • (1) 8" x 38" (F) • (1) 8" x 30 ½" (B) • (4) 8" x 23" (C)
Queen	
(1) 50 ½" x WOF strip, subcut into: • (1) 50 ½" x 40 ½" (A) **(9) 10 ½" x WOF strips, subcut into:** • (4) 10 ½" x 40 ½" (E) • (4) 10 ½" x 35 ½" (D) • (1) 10 ½" x 10 ½"	**(7) 10 ½" x WOF strips, subcut into:** • (1) 10 ½" x 40 ½" (B) • (4) 10 ½" x 30 ½" (C) • (2) 10 ½" x 25 ½" (F)

BACKING // *If you are using this quilt as a backing, you can cut the D and E pieces slightly larger (1"-2") than the other strips so you can have extra fabric on the back of your quilt.*

Assembly

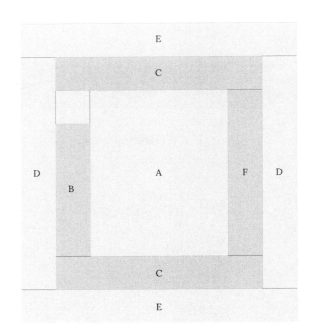

Side 2

1. Sew your white 5 ½" x 5 ½" (8" x 8", 10 ½" x 10 ½") square to one end of your pink B rectangle. Press seam open. Subunit should measure 5 ½" x 25 ½" (8" x 38", 10 ½" x 50 ½"). Sew this strip to the left side of your A rectangle (Diagram 6). Press seams open to form the beginning of your center unit. Subunit should measure 25 ½" x 25 ½" (38" x 38", 50 ½" x 50 ½").

2. Sew the pink F rectangle* to the right side of your center unit (Diagram 7). Press seam open. Subunit should measure 30 ½" x 25 ½" (45 ½" x 38", 60 ½" x 50 ½").

   *Prior to sewing the queen pink F rectangle to right, sew two F rectangles together along the short edges to create a rectangle that is 10 ½" x 50 ½".

3. Sew the two pink C rectangles* to the top and bottom of your center unit (Diagram 8). Press seam open. Subunit should measure 30 ½" x 35 ½" (45 ½" x 53", 60 ½" x 70 ½").

   *Prior to sewing the twin and queen pink C rectangles to the top or bottom, sew two C rectangles together along the short edges to create a rectangle that is 8" x 45 ½" (10 ½" x 60 ½").

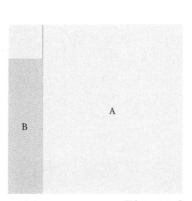

Diagram 6

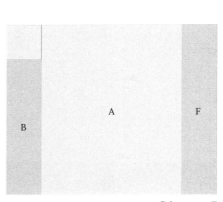

Diagram 7

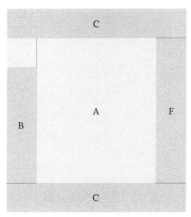

Diagram 8

4. Sew the two white D rectangles* to the left and right of the center unit (Diagram 9). Press seams open. The Subunit should measure 40 ½" x 35 ½" (60 ½" x 53", 80 ½" x 70 ½").

*Prior to sewing the twin and queen white D rectangles to the left or right, sew two D rectangles along the short edges to create a rectangle that is 8" x 53" (10 ½" x 70 ½").

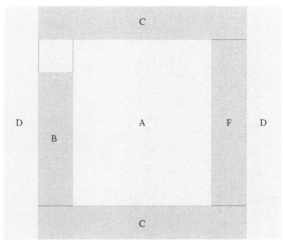

Diagram 9

5. Sew the two white E rectangles* to the top and bottom of your center unit (Diagram 10). Press seams open to finish your top! Finished quit top should measure 40 ½" x 45 ½" (60 ½" x 68", 80 ½" x 90 ½").

*Prior to sewing the twin and queen white E rectangles to the top or bottom, sew two E rectangles along the short edges to create a rectangle that is 8" x 60 ½" (10 ½" x 80 ½").

MAKING THE BACKING // If
you are using this quilt as the backing for Side 1, you can leave the top untrimmed here. This will make it easier to align the quilt sandwich during basting, and it will also give you extra room to square up after you're finished quilting.

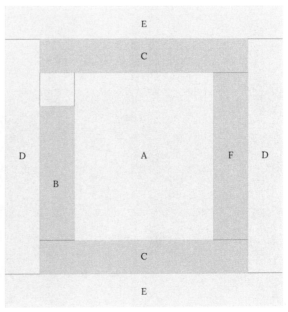

Diagram 10

SIMPLY CREATE // In addition to being inspired by home, Hearth Side 2 is also inspired by the Japanese symbol, ensō. This Zen Buddhist circle is usually hand-drawn with calligraphy, and it represents the moment when the mind is free to let the body simply create. This is one of my favorite quilts to make when I want to just let go and enjoy the process.

*YOU CAN'T BUY HAPPINESS,
BUT YOU CAN BUY A GOOD BOOK
AND ENOUGH FABRIC AND THREAD
TO MAKE A QUILT. SOMETIMES
THAT'S ALL IT TAKES.*

SWAY

Sway

Sway is inspired by dancing and running and moving and playing and creating and expressing oneself. It's about making do, having fun and letting go. I made this quilt with some of the leftovers from other quilts in the book, just for fun. I liked it so much I reverse engineered it for a pattern, and it's now one of my favorite quilts. It's a good reminder to just let go and never underestimate the power of play.

SWAY SIDE 1 // *Materials*

	WHITE	GRAY	BACKING	BINDING
Crib: 33 ½" x 38 ½"	½ yard	¾ yard	1 ¼ yards	½ yard (4 strips)

This quilt is double-sided, and you can use the Side 2 instructions on page 156 for the other side. If you'd rather make a traditional quilt, the backing yardage is indicated above

Cutting Instructions

	WHITE	GRAY
Crib	**(1) 14" x WOF strip**	**(1) 14" x WOF strip** **(1) 10 ½" x WOF strip, subcut into:** • (1) 10 ½" x 39"

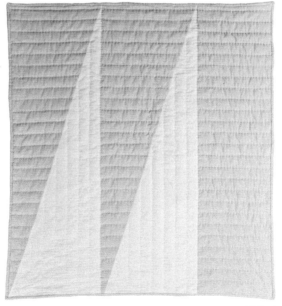

Side 1

Side 2

Assembly

1. Stack the white and gray 14" x WOF strips. Trim the selvages and make rectangles 42" in length.

2. Use a long ruler or a tape measure to mark a diagonal line from the lower left corner to the top right corner. Cut along this line so you create two white and two gray triangles.

3. Pair one white triangle unit to its complementary gray triangle unit. Make sure the white triangle points up toward the right (Diagram 1). Stack these two pieces right sides together, centered over each other and offset by ½" (Diagram 2). Pin generously and sew on the diagonal to make a half-rectangle triangle (HRT) (Diagram 3). Repeat with the other triangle units to make a second HRT unit. Press seams open.

4. Trim the width to 12 ¼", making sure to trim an equal amount from each side. Evenly trim each side so the length is 39".

5. Assemble the quilt top by sewing the two HRTs and remaining gray 10 ½" x 39" rectangle together as shown in Diagram 4. Press seams open. Finished quilt top should measure 34" x 39".

Side 1

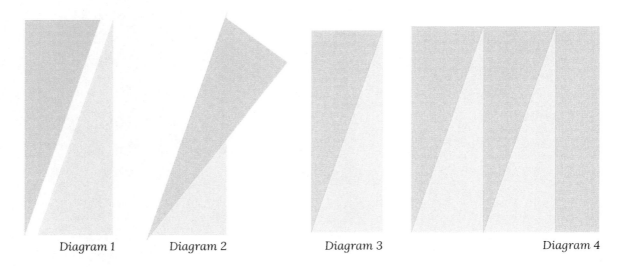

| Diagram 1 | Diagram 2 | Diagram 3 | Diagram 4 |

SWAY SIDE 2 // *Materials*

	WHITE	GRAY	BACKING	BINDING
Crib: 33 ½" x 38 ½"	1 ¼ yard	¾ yard	1 ¼ yards	½ yard (4 strips)

This quilt is double-sided, and you can use the Side 1 instructions on page 154 for the other side.
If you'd rather make a traditional quilt, the backing yardage is indicated above.

Cutting Instructions

WHITE	GRAY
(1) 11 ½" x WOF strip, subcut into: • (1) 11 ½" x 14 ½" **(3) 6 ½" x WOF strips, subcut into:** • (6) 6 ½" x 17" **(1) 6" x WOF strip, subcut into:** • (1) 6" x 39"	**(3) 6 ½" x WOF strips, subcut into:** • (6) 6 ½" x 17"

Crib

Side 2

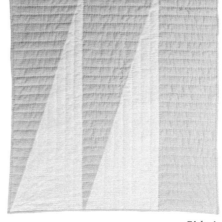

Side 1

Assembly

Side 2

1. Stack one white 6 ½" x 17" rectangle on top of one gray 6 ½" x 17" rectangle and make a diagonal cut from the lower left corner to the upper right corner.

2. Pair one white triangle unit to its complementary gray triangle unit. Make sure the white triangle points up toward the right (Diagram 1, pg. 155). Stack these two pieces right sides together, centered over each other and offset by ½" (Diagram 2, pg. 155). Pin generously and sew on the diagonal to make an HRT (Diagram 3, pg. 155). Repeat Steps 1 and 2 to make 12 HRT units. Press seams open.

3. Trim the HRT width to 6", making sure to trim an equal amount from each side. Evenly trim so the length is 14 ½".

4. Sew five HRT units together as shown in Diagram 5. Press seams open. Subunit should measure 14 ½" x 28".

5. Sew a separate column of seven units together as shown in Diagram 6. Press seams open. Subunit should measure 14 ½" x 39".

6. Sew the 14 ½" x 11 ½" white rectangle to the bottom of your five-piece HRT column. Press seam open. Subunit should measure 14 ½" x 39".

7. Assemble the rest of the quilt top as shown in Diagram 7 to finish. Press seams open. Finished quilt top should measure 34" x 39".

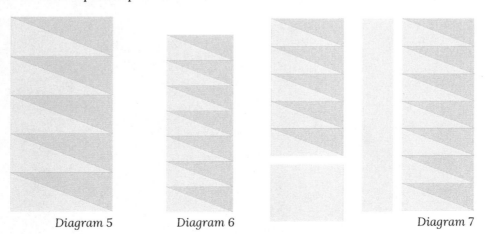

Diagram 5   Diagram 6   Diagram 7

*BY MAKING QUILTS, WE PRESERVE THE TRADITION
OF SO MANY WHO CAME BEFORE US.*

*BY MAKING QUILTS OUR OWN, WE CARRY
IT ON FOR THE NEXT GENERATION.*

ACKNOWLEDGMENTS

There are so many incredible people who helped make this book a reality, and they deserve my deepest gratitude. To Jen Geigley, who graciously agreed to meet a stranger for coffee and tell her everything about self publishing. Jen, your advice has been invaluable on this journey, and I'm forever grateful (and forever a fan of your work). To Kristen Lee of Mashe Modern for helping provide the gorgeous fabric in this book. Your light and energy inspire me daily. To Jessie, for the batting, the dinner dates and for dragging me into the amazing community of quilters in central Iowa. I came for #quiltyourhair, and I stayed because you are an amazing human being. To Carol and Erin, for being my sounding board, keeping it real, and being some of the best quilty friends a girl could ask for. I am so honored to be part of your lives.

To Austin and Lauren for letting my quilts in to your life and home. You are true wizards and I'm in awe of your talent and generosity. To Nyah, Nadia, Ellie and Esmae, thank you for making this book beautiful with your grace, laughter and gorgeous smiles. To Yvonne, for taking my sad quilt math and turning it into something worth trusting. To my sister, Erin, who made this book beautiful and worked with me patiently for so many nights. It was an honor to make this book with you. Thank you, forever, for everything.

To Heather, Alissa, Molly, Amanda and Elizabeth, for being strong and inspiring forces in my life. (And to Amanda for your eagle eyes.) I don't know who I'd be if I'd never met and worked with y'all. To my parents, for teaching me to be mentally tough and never quit what you've started. I'm here because of you, in so many ways. To Deb, for being my cheerleader, mentor, confidant and teacher. You set me rightly on so many paths, I am forever in your debt. To Jess, for giving me a chance and being the nicest person I know.

To my grandma for teaching me to quilt. I didn't know how important it was when we were making that first quilt together. So much has changed, but I will never forget those days hunched over patterns and scrap bins in your basement. And to my grandpa for "inspecting" our work — and making sure the pool was ready when we needed a break.

And to Kevin. Thank you for being the first to look at my work (and for saying it's great, every time). Thank you for believing in me, pushing me, building spreadsheets and brainstorming with me over so many margaritas. You are the best, and these quilts are for us. (And of course Dal, who uses them more than anyone.)

About the Author

Riane Menardi Morrison is a modern quilter and designer making minimal quilts for the modern home. She learned to quilt in 2011 from her grandmother, and when she discovered modern quilts, linen fabric, and sashiko thread, she fell in love and never looked back.

Riane is a coauthor of the book *Modern Quilts: Designs of the New Century* by the Modern Quilt Guild, and her quilts have been featured in numerous magazines and quilt exhibits. She teaches and lectures on hand quilting and modern quilt design around the country and practices yoga in her spare time. Riane lives with her husband, Kevin, and silly pup, Dallas.

Connect online at riane-elise.com or on Instagram @riane.elise.

Made in the USA
Las Vegas, NV
14 November 2023

80831049R00102